T0365030

ISSUES -
of the World
of the United States

Robert William Kupp

Order this book online at www.trafford.com
or email orders@trafford.com

Most Trafford titles are also available at major online book retailers.

Print information available on the last page.

ISBN: 978-1-4907-7448-0 (sc)
ISBN: 978-1-4907-7450-3 (hc)
ISBN: 978-1-4907-7449-7 (e)

Library of Congress Control Number: 2016909979

Trafford rev.   07/19/2016

PUBLISHING®   www.trafford.com
North America & international
toll-free: 1 888 232 4444 (USA & Canada)
fax: 812 355 4082

Contents

Tables

Tables

Prologue

- **Issues** - n - A point of discussion, debate, dispute, or a matter of public concern

Most books dealing with issues of the World or United States are usually written by "Experts" and are narrowly focused on a particular issue - e.g. Population, Food, Global Warming, Economy, Terrorists, etc. I have attempted in this book to cover many of these issues as a lay person, albeit as an engineer and scientists who has done a lot of reading, thinking and worrying about the many issues of the World and of the United States. In my prior book I narrowly focused on "Energy", its future but not its World consequences. Here I hope to develop the background, status and my view of the future, good and bad, for many/most of the issues, problems, disasters, that the World and the United States currently face.

Some of the major issues are more applicable to the whole World – Population, Food, and Water. Others are both the World and the United States – Global Warming, National and World Economies, Terrorism, Religion. There are other issues that are of greater concern to the United States – Inequality and Economic Distribution, Unemployment and Under-Employment, Terrorism – particularly if the terrorists stole a nuclear weapon.

My arbitrary distribution of issues between World and the United States is not embedded in stone as essentially all of them could be considered of World-wide importance. I believe maintaining some separation helps in the discussion of their affect and possible solutions, or at least mitigation.

Before discussing the issues, it is first necessary to understand the World, and its many Nations, as related to population, social trends and to its industrial development. This brings us to Chapter One - "Current World Status".

Chapter 1

Current World Status

The World's future is primarily a function of only a few key determinants-

- **Population** –
  1.6 billion in1900 – 6.0 in 2000 – 11.2 in 2100?

- **Standard of Living** –
  Effects everything – personally and nationally

- **Environment** -
  Global Warming, Water, Land, Flora and Fauna

Independent of population, how nations deal with various issues, depends on that nation's current, living standard, educational level (intelligence), economic status, industrial development, governmental policy or form of government, and in some cases religion. One of the most important of these is the industrial status or level of development, as this affects wealth, food, energy consumption, and that nation's monetary ability to cope with many different issues.

On "Environment", there is is a fundamental conflict between the "Have" and "Have-not" nations specifically on global warming. The "Haves" are the current major contributor to the warming gases, while the have-nots are a key to the future for as they grow, both in population and in energy demand, they will contribute more to global warming and its problems.

One of the recognized measurements of the "Standard of Living" is that of total energy consumption per capital. The nation's "Gross Domestic Product" is also considered to be such a guide line by many economists. In my view GDP measures many functions which do no directly relate to the individuals living standard, e.g. Wall Street. Energy consumption is a clear measure of the factors which determine how people live – Income, Wealth, Food, Housing, Transportation as well as the "Extras" – TV, Entertainment, Books, Hobbies and the list goes on.

Energy – A Standard of Living

There a several approaches that have been used to quantify total energy use which include – Equivalent Barrels of Oil, Kilowatt-hours of Electricity, Tons of Coal. A difficulty with all of these measurement approaches are that they result in huge numbers, many zeros, and are therefore difficult for the mind to keep in perspective or compare. The unit that I prefer is designated by the letter $\mathbf{Q}$, which stands for quads, or 10^{15} (One with 15 zeros after it) British Thermal Units. A BTU is a measure of heat, and all forms of energy can be converted to heat. Specifically, one BTU is the amount of energy required to raise one pound of water (two cups) one degree Fahrenheit – not much energy and that is why $\mathbf{Q}$ is 10^{15}. With this background, Table 1 summarizes how this $\mathbf{Q}$ value is distributed around many regions of the World.

Table 1

Regions of the World Q Values - 2010

Region	Population Billions	Q per Billion	Q Total
World	6.8	75	510
USA	**0.3**	**330**	**99**
Germany	0.1	170	14
Japan	0.13	180	23
China	1.4	74	104
India	1.2	20	24
South America	0.5	22	11
Africa	1.0	14	4

This ratio, **Q** per Billion People, correlates well with a classical definition of a nation's wealth as well as characterizing the financial and living standard of the people. Table 2 summarizes a typical definition of **Q** values as related to the industrial development of nations. It should be noted that all of these numbers are rough estimates, as all such measurements have errors, are done by different organizations, and at different times and hence are difficult to correlate. Even rough estimates are useful tools in thinking about the issues and debating about a difference of 10%, or even 20% is a diversion.

Table 2

A Nation's Standard of Living

Q per Billion People

300 **Q**/B	Technological Man - Current USA
100 **Q**/B	Industrial Man - USA 1900
42 **Q**/B	Advanced Agricultural Man – USA 1870
17 **Q**/B	Agricultural Man - Pre-machinery

These values of **Q** per billion people are a key to how we can think of the future. All of the nations of the World strive to move upward in the listing – all hoping to achieve the ultimate status of "Technological Man". Even those nations, e.g. United States that have arrived at that goal, still tend to increase their status, as this is an average, and upward mobility continues as the lower segments of the population strive for a better life.

Another key factor in developing the future issues and status of the World is the population, both current and projecting that growth into the future. The whole World totals are important for many issues, e.g. total food supply, water, land for farming, unique mineral resources and of course energy consumption. These, as well as many other factors are even more specifically applicable to individual nations and will be discussed in much detail later in this book.

An issue that affects every nation and continents of the World is that dealing with the environment. Global Warming is such an issue, a huge concern, and will be covered in a separate chapter.

Chapter 2

Population - The World and the United States

Population is the driving force for many of the current issues in the World, both current and more importantly – the future. It is apparent that population demands determine the need for the many resources that individuals and society demand. The list goes on forever, but some of the more important topics include:

- Food - Certainly the most important
- Water - Personal, Agricultural, Industrial
- Land - To live on and to grow food
- Mineral Resources - Needed for manufacturing
- Energy - "Standard of Living"-Table 2
- Global Warming – Energy, but from where?

There are essentially three groups of countries in which population and growth is ether; not an issue, is of concern, or is already a disaster and getting worse. The highly industrial nations, the United States, the Western European group, Japan all have a population that is generally under control and will continue that way for at least the near term future.

The two most populist nations, India and China, are characteristic of this second group but there is a major difference between them. India, with a population of 1.2 billion still has a moderate growth rate and a significant rising demand from an increase in the standard of living. China, with a population of 1.4 billion, has a rising standard of living demand but seems to have population growth under control. It should be noted that they recently change the "Requirement" of one child per family to allow for two, which will result in a stable population level.

The third group: Sub-Sahara Africa, South Asia, Latin America, East Africa, have a large population, a total on the order of 2 billion, with an extremely high growth rate, and an major demand for an increase in the standard of living. Many nations in this group are not even into the "Advance Agricultural Man" of Table 2

Population Futures

In order to quantify the issues related to population Table 3 summarizes the projected growth of the regions of the World as developed by the United Nations. This is their "Median" values and after the table, the upper "limits", a scary prediction is discussed.

Table 3

Future Regional Population

Year	World	Asia	Africa	Europe	LatinA	NA
	Billions					
2015	7.3	4.4	1.2	0.7	0.6	0.4
2030	8.4	4.9	1.6	0.7	0.7	0.4
2050	9.6	5.2	2.4	0.7	0.8	0.4
2080	10.5	5.0	3.6	0.6	0.8	0.5
2100	11.2	4.7	4.2	0.6	0.8	0.5
Increase	3.9	0.3	3.0	-0.1	0.1	0.1

The possible range in projections to the year 2100 is wide. A "Low" UN estimate is essentially no change, although it is a slight decrease to 7.0 billion. The "High" is nearly unbelievable at 17.0 billion, an increase a 10 billion – more than double the current level. This high estimate basically assumes that the World population will continue to grow at the current rate, a very pessimistic and unlikely view of the future.

It can be noted from the table that nearly all of the population increase is in Africa. This is particularly worrisome for, as shown in Table 1 and Table 2, this continent is currently in the "Pre-machinery" age. Hence as they grow in population they will certainly also trend to up their energy status and Gross Domestic Product which will add an incredibly burden to World resources – food, natural resources, energy, etc.

It is useful to add to the population predictions how these regions will also increase their Standard of Living - e.g. GDP as measured by **Q**. This is much more speculative, but considering the wide range developed for the population predictions this cannot be that far wrong. Further, it is necessary to develop such data to adequately consider the future of the World. At least we know that all nations will trend upward, so that the **Q** per billion people will tend to rise – more in the undeveloped Nations but also in others, but to a lesser extent.

Future Energy

With these caveats, Table 4 has been developed and for convenience of comparison the data from Table 1 are included with their Gross Domestic Product as indicated by total energy – **Q**. Contrary to the usual situation that all **Q** per person values increase you will note that the USA decreases from 330 in 2010 to 290 for 2100. This decrease is based on the apparent fact that America is now at the top of the chain but that the country will continue to improve efficiency in manufacturing and energy use, both domestic and commercial. Europe, China, India all have had significant growth but the largest increases are for undeveloped regions, South America and primarily Africa. Africa is most important because their population growth rate is near the highest in the World – as noted nearly all of the World's population increase from 2016 to 2100 is in this region.

Part of this continued growth in Africa is the imbedded tradition and culture. Large families are revered in the African nations, eight or ten children per family, and this was historically a requirement for life. Many children and adults died as a result of the diseases and illnesses caused by bad water, malnutrition and inadequate medical care. Further, children were needed for the family farm – which provides most of their food. In the modern age the number of children per family has been going down but it is still high by World standards. Tradition is hard to change.

Table 4

Future Q Value Estimates

2100 Estimate

Region	Population Billions	Q per Billion	Q Total
World	11.2	88	985
USA	**0.4**	**290**	**116**
Europe	0.6	200	120
China	1.0	60	102
India	1.7	180	180
South America	0.6	60	36
Africa	4.2	40	168

2010 For Reference

Region	Population Billions	Q per Billion	Q Total
World	6.8	75	510
USA	**0.3**	**330**	**99**
Europe	0.6	123	74
China	1.4	74	104
India	1.3	20	24
South America	0.5	22	11
Africa	1.0	14	14

I commented above that the upper limit of the World population growth is a scary, 17 billion people – 230% increase from today. If, for illustration, it is assumed that this increased population's status would be at a 88 Q per billion level (the World average estimate for 2100 in the above table) the total energy for the word would be 1,500

Q. This is roughly three times the current value. This would be catastrophic when you think about, food, resources, land, and particularly global warming. These many issues will be addressed in the following chapters.

Projections into the future, particularly the far future – 2100, are invariably wrong as there are many factors which will cause changes that are unpredictable. Think how far off Thomas Robert Malthus was in his ultimate limits to the World's population. When the World had about one billion people, in 1789, he postulated that the exponential growth in population would relatively soon out-strip food supply – farmers can not keep up with the population's requirements. At the current World population at 7.3 billion we are along way from 1789, and only a relatively few people are starving. though many are undernourished. Will Malthusian philosophy apply to the current rapid population growth in Africa – a region with current food shortages? The UN has estimated that Africa will be the major population growth region of the World and even that estimate assumes there will be some reduction in family size, and hopefully with improved education the logic of birth control that could certainly happen.

One final thought on population is the concept, or perhaps scientific basis, for how large a population the earth is able to permanently support. This thought is highly debatable, but many scientists believe that when you consider the continuing degradation of the resources of the World – lowering of water tables, depletion of farm land yields, and even the washing away of farm land, at 7.3 billion we are already too large. Some social scientists have the opinion that about 5 billion would be a good limit. The long term future will determine who is correct.

Chapter 3

Food

From prehistoric times to the present food and water are the key requirements to the survival of mankind, or for that mater, all other animals. Water, per se, will be discussed later, but food is a major World issue. It is debatable as to which comes first – population or food, but the two are directly related.

Thomas Robert Malthus in his book, "Essay on the Principle of Population" - published in 1789, was the first to relate and be concerned with the direct relationship between population and food. At the time the World, with a population of roughly one billion people, was still in the "Advanced Agricultural Man" stage – no machine farming. With the invention of a more practical steam engine by James Watt in 1781 the "Industrial Age" was beginning and rapidly expanding so that this major industrial development could not have been for seen by Malthus. He had the firm opinion that the World population would be limited by the food supply. He did not believe in birth control but thought that by marrying later, and with many earlier deaths due to malnutrition, disease, war, and famine population would be controlled.

Current Status

Now with 7.3 billion people in the World, and not too many dying of starvation, why was Malthus wrong? Two "new" conditions contribute to mitigate his conclusions.

- The Industrial Age – The giant, and smaller, diesel and gas driven machines (Plows, Harvesters, Processors) and other industrial technologies (Irrigation, Fertilizers) have increased a farmers productivity by many multiples from tens to hundreds.

- The Technological Age – The crops have changed historically by selective improvements and more recently by genetic modification. The yield per acre has been dramatically increased the use of man-made fertilizers, new pesticides, soil management, irrigation and optimizing the crop to the location.

These two bullets summarize the current key developments but some of the details are both informative and interesting. One of the early and simple improvements was the invention of the steel plow by John Deere in 1837. It greatly improved the speed and depth of plowing and it required significantly less energy. The company he formed went on to develop some of the most complicated farm machines that do everything that hundreds of individuals previously had to perform.

Typically, a single machine has the capability to, harvest, separate, clean, and finally load the crop into passing trucks. The trucks then bring this partially prepared food to the processing plant and where more automated machines further sort, clean, cook preserve and package the food for final distribution to the public. This very efficient mechanized process replaced the hundreds of people

14

originally needed before the machine age became the key and major step in feeding the World.

The concept of optimizing a crop to a location has been around for a long time. It was obvious to even earliest farmers that some crops need more water, others did better if the soil was richer, and others tolerate less rain. Even average temperature has shown to have an important effect on the crop. For example, optimum average temperatures for best growth are roughly 59°F for wheat, 64°F for maize, 72°F for soy beans, and 74°F for rice. This latter example will be of even more importance as global warming continues and farming will probably have to adjust to different crops and perhaps move geographically.

As the food requirements of the World change in the future, how much more of an improvement in farming can be considered, or even necessary? A most critical input into future food needs relate to those nations with the largest populations, India, China, and in the future Africa. As these nations strive toward the "Technological Age", their food "Requirement" will certainly change. The USA can be considered the ultimate limit to such a change with a diet high in meat and calories per-capita with the consequential result of a farming technology (energy, land, machinery) that is many times that of developing nations

All of the above improvements, machine driven farming, improved crops, fertilizing, and pest protection, indicate that World food production could be very substantially increased. There is a question, a restricting factor, as many of these changes are brought about by the huge farming corporations, and these corporations are not driven by the "need for more global food" but by short term corporate economics - "Will this major investment produce a near term increase in profitability?" This brings us to a key factor in food production, the ability of the people to buy it – the relationship between poverty and food.

15

Food and Income

Among the poor of the World, 60% of the family income is required for the purchase of food. This number changes dramatically as the nation comes into the "Technological Age". For example, the United States spends a total of about 10% of their income on food with only 6% for home consumption and 4% of this total is away, restaurants, fast food, and snacks. However, for the poor, the 60% of their spending does not amount to very much money as would be necessary to develop greater production infrastructure.

The extreme poor are currently defined as having an income of on $1.25 per day per person and there are about 1.4 billion people in the World at this level. Their location is primarily in South Asia and Sub-Sahara Africa. This level of poverty obviously brings on malnutrition which further greatly increases illnesses and many times starvation. Surprisingly there has bean an incredible improvement in poverty over the eons - two centuries ago 95% of the population was considered to be in extreme poverty, versus the 20% today. Poverty doesn't stop at $1.25 per day as $2.50 per day is the income of half the people of the World, still poor but not quite as destitute. In a subsequent chapter "Inequality" will be further discussed.

This low level of income has a result that in Sub-Sahara Africa 23% of the population are seriously undernourished or starving. This is reduced to about 10% for the World and to less than 5% in developed nations and with no starving. As an aside, even in the richest nation, America, with no significant dollar restriction for the purchase of food, large fractions of the population do not eat healthy. Everyone gets enough calories to the extent that two thirds of the people are either overweight or obese.

So with all this prior discussion, what does the future in food look like? For the next 10 or 20 years we can probably muddle through without too much of a change. The two most populous nations, China and India, are continuing to improve their economy and hence their standard of living, so the food supply will go along with it. China particularly, with their continuing significant economic growth, albeit with ups and downs, can probably attract or develop the giant food producing corporations to help feed the World, and to go upward in their own standards – greater variation and more protein.

Africa is different, for as noted above the natives are too poor, and as far as new production goes – it's sort of a "Chicken and Egg" situation. There is not enough money to buy more food and with that being the case there is no incentive to invest in greater productivity or production machinery. There is a possibility that because Africa has potentially developable farm lands that could be attractive to the food corporations, particularly as farmland or water become less available in the rest of the World.

The fully developed nations, much of Europe and the United States, have some issues but certainly no significant food problem in both the near term, and probably the long term.

The Future

One of the problems in the advanced as well as developing nations is food waste. About one third of all the food produced, grown, never gets to the household to be eaten and even when it gets there another 20% is uneaten and discarded. Less than half the food grown is actually consumed. The 53% lost is roughly as follows: Lost at the farm - 20%; Storage and shipping – 3%; Production, packaging, canning – 2%; Wholesalers -Supermarkets discard – 9%; Home waste – 19%.

Better management of this waste could feed many millions of the poor. At the farm, for example malformed carrots, potatoes, etc., although fully edible, are disposed of as they cannot be sold. Some cities are organizing a collection and distribution system to recover these food losses and deliver them to the needy, but this amounts to only a small fraction of the losses. There could be more. Some of this lost is partially saved as animal feed – the pigs love it.

The World's out look, particularly the poorest and growing nations, has a greater concern for the far future. These nations, as reviewed above, currently have a large fraction of their people that are ether undernourished or starving. As population is increased from the present 1.2 billion in Africa to an estimate 4.2 billion in 2100, nearly triple the size there must be major increases in food supply or the there will be massive starvation. This food supply in Africa, which is now marginal, must increase by at least a factor of three and hopefully to four or even five by the end of the century. There is some undeveloped land that has a good potential for farming but entrepreneurial development is a requirement. Considering the business philosophy, "Profit - not Need", of large investors, the corporate food giants, such needed expansion may not happen. If it does not, the current level of malnutrition, disease, and starvation in Africa will only get worse. There will be more on these relationships in a subsequent chapter on economics. The other critical factor for food production is water, discussed in the next chapter.

Chapter 4

Water

Water is absolutely needed for man and society to survive for three reasons-

- Personal use – For drinking, cooking, cleaning and in more erudite regions – watering the grass. With out drinking water you will survive for about five days
- Farming – Food will not grow, or food animals will die without water, either rain or irrigation
- Manufacturing – Man survived for tens of thousands of years without this function, but our current World requires a lot of water

Consumption Rates

It might be interesting to know how much water we current consume, both for individuals and for a nation. As you would expect, the per capita consumption for all of the three uses above varies dramatically from country to country. An overall measurement basis is the total water withdrawn per capital per day and this goes from a high in the United States of 1,200 gallons per day per capita, to about 300-400 g/d/c in most of Europe and this volume drops to a low of around 50 in Sub-Sahara Africa. You will note that United States is 25 times higher than Africa. When all the nations of the World are averaged together the daily withdrawals from all sources is 340 gallons per day.

These same kind of ratios exist for personal water use with US again being high a with about 150 gallons per day and Africa at only 5 gallons per day, and most of the African waters are not clean.

These data are sort of interesting but they do not develop an issue or a concern per se. To understand the consequences of the above, the total water consumption of the World has to be examined and where that water comes from. Finally, are there enough sources to supply the needs of a growing population and an expanding World economy?

The first number to consider is how much water is withdrawn for human use in the whole World? One unit of measurement for this water that is not too large for the mind to consider is 3,900 km^3, that's cubic kilometers – a huge amount of water. Why not talk about a measurement that everyone knows – gallons? If we convert the above 3,900 km^3 to gallons the number would be huge - 900,000,000,000,000, that's a 9 with 14 zeros after it - clearly not an easy number to think about, and if you want to say it - nine hundred trillion. This quantity of water is used primarily for farming, 2,700 km^3 - about 70%. The second use is industry at 700 km^3 - 19%, and finally the remainder is for personal use at about 10%.

Sources of Water

There are only two sources for this human requirement, surface water – freshwater lakes or rivers, and groundwater – that which is pumped out of the ground in both shallow and deep wells. All of these water sources originate from World precipitation – rain and snow. There is an incredible amount of precipitation that falls on the earth, 117,000 km^3 – that's about 30 times the amount we currently use. So, is there a problem about the future? First, 71% of the precipitation falls into the oceans and another significant fraction falls as snow in the Artic and Antarctic regions. The rain forest precipitation drains into high flowing rivers, e.g. the Amazon, and into the ocean, where nearly all of the water on the earth exists. Actually over 97% of all the water in the World is saline, salty, and is not useful for most human needs. This ocean can be converted to fresh water but only at huge costs, only sustainable in a few unusual situations, and not for irrigation.

Most of the fresh water of the earth is unavailable to humans as it is as it is frozen in polar ice caps and glaciers, or in unavailable ground water. Nearly all of the fresh water the World is currently consuming comes from rivers and a little from lakes. These sources represent only one-half of one percent of the fresh water on the earth and are pretty well tapped by the nations of the World.

The fact that nearly all of fresh water that countries current use comes from rivers, can represent a major inter-nation, or even within a nation, issue. Most usable rivers in the World pass through several nations and many of these nations do not have treaties or agreements as to how the water flowing through their country should be shared. As the nations upstream Gross Domestic Product grows, and its water requirements increase, they take more water from the river as it flows through their boundaries leaving less for the downstream nations - a major conflict as to who "Owns" the water. In the United States the Rio Grand is a case in point. In dryer years by the time it flows to Mexico it is hardly flowing, and even before that, several States are fighting over water rights. Such conflicts have been going on for centuries – remember the "Old West" and

21

the cowboy gun battles over – "Who owns the water in the creek?"

When you do not have enough water, where or how do you get it? – You can either "Pipe" it in from some more remote location, or you drill for it. Both methods have been around for a long time. The incredibly engineered Roman Aqueducts which supplied the huge city of old Rome are World famous and can still be seen eons later. Historically water wells were shallow and collected near surface ground water, on the order of dozens of feet deep. In undeveloped counties they are still used, complete with a hand crank to raise the pail.

Modern wells are deeper, hundreds of feet, if you are lucky, to many thousands. In western United States, with the drought of the past several years and the lack of surface water, farmers have been drilling deeper and deeper to pump up the water needed for their crops. This has caused a modern water war, as this drilling not only lowers the water table at the well site but can also lower it below the neighboring farmers well so he is out of water. It is the same argument as above on a nations river water rights and the cow boy gun fights over the local creek.

There is a more fundamental issue resulting from this deeper and deeper drilling and that is the permanent loss of that water resource. Water aquifers are formed and maintained by rain on the surface and the gradual seepage of that water down to the water table, a process that may take from hundreds to thousands of years. If you pump out more than this annual seepage it results in a lowering of the water table and the ultimate loss - an irreplaceable water resource. That is where western United States and many regions of the World are going. This is not only irresponsible, but in the not too distant future an unsustainable source of needed water.

Future Sources

The need for more water must therefore come from surface sources – rivers, but where? Unfortunately, the World has used up much of the nearby rivers and hence more and longer aqueducts are needed – do the Romans one better, and is there enough in those rivers. As noted above, the World is currently withdrawing 3,900 km³ of water and for comparison the total water flow from all of the significant rivers of the world is about 37,000 km³. In round number we currently consume about 10% of that flowing in all of the rivers – clearly enough water, but again the problem is "Where?" Some of the largest rivers of the World, the Amazon, the Congo, which have a total flow of over 8,000 km³, 22% of the Worlds, are not near population and this is the case for many other lesser rivers.

In order to optimally use river water, it is usually required the build a dam. This not only develops a long lake for a reserve supply in the dry season, but also raise the height of the water so it can flow by gravity to the farms and cities where needed. An ultimate example of this is the construction of the Grand Coulee Dam on the Columbia River in the State of Washington. Construction started in 1935 and after several design changes was completed in 1942. At a mile long and 550 feet high it backed up a lake 150 miles long, to nearly the Canadian border. This water reservoir provides farm irrigation for more 400,000 square miles. As an aside, to be discussed later in the Energy chapter, the dam also generates over 6,000 megawatts of power, the largest single power station in the United States.

Both of these dam functions, irrigation and power, have been built by the tens of thousands all over the World, but not to such a grand scale. China has had, and continues to plan, one of the more massive dam building programs on the earth. Since 1950 they have constructed about 22,000 dams of 50 feet or more in height. On a totally different

23

scale the Three Gorges Dam on the Yangtze River has now been recently completed. This massive structure replaces the Grand Coulee record, with a height of 600 feet, a length of not quite a mile and a half, and having a power generating capacity of 22,000 megawatts. Its primary purpose is not irrigation but power, navigation on the river, and flood control. The flood control does have a farming function as the periodic flooding of the Yangtze has been a serious problem with farming in the region. Chinas future construction is also ambitious. To provide the added water and power necessary to support their growing economy and farming requirements they have plans to build 130 large dams by 2020.

As dams are built for irrigation throughout the World there will be serious and possibly deadly arguments between nations. As noted above, many useable rivers flow through several nations and as these dams divert more water to that nation's farm land the next nation down stream will most certainly object – and this would lead to confrontation and as the situation becomes desperate - possibly to a local war.

At the beginning of the chapter it was noted that 70% of water requirements are for farming – the growing of food. The most desperate region of the World with a serious food shortage is Sub-Sahara Africa. This region is also among the lowest in the World for water withdrawal per capita, and for personal use. The Congo River, one of the largest on earth, has all and more than would be needed, but it has to be moved to the people and future farms. This requires entrepreneurs and capital, not too available in Africa. It is certainly conceivable that Africa, some land suitable for farming and natural water availability, will eventually be "Discovered". The only question is "When?"- And how many more people and children will be undernourished and die before this happens. Unfortunately, this same pattern exists in many poor regions of the World.

Chapter 5

Economics

Economics is a scary subject for most people to deal with so I will try to keep it at a lay level. It is the general philosophy of most economists that for a viable future, both for the nations, its people, and for the World, that there must be growth in the economy – hence a continuing increase in "Gross Domestic Product" which will hopefully, but not necessarily, will rub off, trickle down, on the people and increase their standard of living.

Economic Growth

The "not necessarily" caveat needs a comment. Consider the United States economic development of the past 40 years. Its economy as measured by the Gross Domestic Product has increased by 94% - that is an average of 1.6% per year, not an overwhelming growth rate but this rate does produce a very significant increase in a long period of time. The distribution of this extra growth is shocking and has been commented to in many articles of the past few years. Most of this doubling of wealth has gone to the top 1% of the people with their income increasing 200%. The lower 80% went up only 45%, and the lower 20% did not go up at all - so much for the GDP as a determinant of the economic health of the nation, at least as related to the inequality of people.

A nation's economic growth has two components, the first being dependent on population per se, and the second being a growth in individual productivity – how much GDP can one worker produce. The difference between these two is critical to the status of the individual. The first, if GDP increases in step with the population the individual share of growth remains unchanged - a status quo. The second, increased productivity, can clearly be to the benefit to the individual, but not necessarily so – the preceding paragraph.

It is the view of most, but not all, economists that the nations and the World must have an ever increasing economy – that is a higher Gross Domestic Product per capita. Such an increase would continue to improve the living standard of all the people of the World. Historically, at least since circa 1870 when the industrial revolution was well underway, this has been the case. In earlier eons, the prior 1800 years, there was very little if any GDP growth per capita, so the concept of the requirement for a perpetual increase is not embedded in stone. As reasonably accurate GDP data have become available growth has been more accurately determined: 1870 – 1920 1.8% per year; 1920 – 1970 a high rate of 2.8%; and in most recent times 1970 – 2014 1.6%. These data are for the United States but are reasonably indicative of the trend in the rest of the industrial World.

Some economists (e.g. Robert J. Gordon) have tried to account for the different rates of GDP growth in these eras so as to better project what will happen in the future, rather than follow the party line - "Growth will/must continue". Simplifying to some degree, the first period, 1870 – 1920, is the direct result of the rapidly expanding technology of the industrial revolution. Think what inventions and technology evolved in this 50 year period. The list goes on forever but the following includes many of the incredibly important developments: Electricity and the electric motor; The internal combustion engine – cars, trucks, and farming machines; Central heating; In house the connection of running water and sewers.

The next 50 years, 1920 -1970 is a little more difficult to justify the increase of a very high growth rate. There was of course the continuing and expanding use of electricity, and its offspring, electronics. Many of us who lived during this period can name the list: Appliances – washing machines, vacuums, dishwashers, microwaves, freezers; Electronics – radio, television, and with silicon chips the main frame computers and the beginning of the personal computer. Another contributor to this high growth rate period was a result of World War II. For growth, capital investment is required, and the massive war effort provided government funded factories and manufacturing equipment which were instantly available at no cost post war. The second contribution was the development of much higher production efficiency during the war, which carried over to the manufacturing of consumer products.

The current era, 1970 – 2014, growth in the GDP dropped back to slightly less than the pre-war history – about 1.6% per year. This percentage increase, considered minimal by many economists, resulted in the doubling of the United States GDP during the period. However, the benefit to the individual only increased by about 30%, as the population increased from 205 million to 318 million. This increase in GDP was shared by an additional 100 million people, but as previously noted the top 1% received most of it.

As stated above, many economists and most politicians believe that the last 40 year's rate of expansion is too low and must be increased, while a few of the economists think the recent history is the norm and may even be too high for the future. In the United States, what may drive the economy to higher values, or conversely why is the growth lower than previous eras? Think about the inventions/developments in the two prior periods sited above, and is it conceivable that the future could duplicate the past.

These past 50 years have been not so much an inventive era, but more of an evolution. There have been negligible new appliances, maybe a robotic vacuum cleaner or an electric tooth brush, but except for the internet and every one having a cell phone, nothing substantive. Automobiles don't go any faster although they are more efficient and automated – a very large number of electric motors to move seats, roll windows, move side-view mirrors, etc. Although not much is new, people are buying more "Stuff" – snow blowers, multiple television sets, two cars per family, and more gadgets. As noted, cell phones have been a development of this era, but already most individuals who want them have them – every couple years there is an "Improvement", but this is not new invention – only a more complicated, smaller, replacement. All of this "Extra" buying does increase the GDP but how long can this go on, and will there be any new inventions which can change the current pattern. No one can predict the future, but in my opinion it would be clearly impossible to duplicate the twentieth century's inventions and the resultant increase in the standard of living for those who can afford these new and newer products.

Distribution of Economic Growth

When you consider the increase in the United States GDP over the past several decades, nearly all of it came from the service industries. Unfortunately, the really useful driving force for a sturdy economy is manufacturing and this sector has been decreasing, becoming a smaller and smaller fraction of the economy. This loss of manufacturing is a major contributor to our large negative balance of payment – we buy too many hard goods from overseas manufactures.

Further, this manufacturing loss has significantly reduced the availability of both intermediate and lower level jobs. This has happened because our labor costs are significantly higher than China and other developing nations. This cheaper off-shore labor has driven many US manufacturers overseas. Import tariffs would help equalize the situation, but would also raise the cost of living. At least two concerns discourage a tariff approach – people screaming about higher costs and the start of a tariff war with an unknown outcome. There has been some modest improvement lately because the introduction of automation and robotics which has made labor costs less important. Of course these new automated manufacturing facilities also require fewer workers – an employment issue.

This loss of manufacturing since 1990 has had a serious impact on the economic health of the United States. There may be greater economic consequences if the manufacturing component of our economy does not return, or at least increase, toward to its historic past levels. To be specific, the US Manufacturing Trade Deficit prior to 1990 was negligible and went up to about $100 billion per year in 1990 and from 2006 to 2010 it has been in the $500 billion range.

This drop in manufacturing is further documented in the employment statistics – from 1970 to 2000, up and down at around 20 million manufacturing jobs, but from 2000 to 2014 a dramatic drop to 12 million. The decrease is even more worrisome when thought of as a percent of the work force. In 1970 manufacturing jobs employed about 19% of the work force and this dropped by 2015 to only 8%. Part of this drop was due to automation and robotics which did dramatically increase productivity per man-hour. There are many more people in the work force today with the largest increase in the service industries – 15 million in 1977 to an incredible 62 million in 2015.

Unemployment - and the Future

A major factor in the United States economy is employment – or more correctly unemployment. Even with the increases in employment in service, transportation and construction industries as well as with more government bureaucracy there is still unemployment and underemployment - many part-timers. We can look to past history as a solution to this problem. In the beginning of the 20th century most workers labored for about 60 hours per week, about the same as in the previous century. As manufacturing became more efficient and labor unions evolved in the first half of the 20th, the work could be accomplished with fewer man-hours and the work week dropped to 40 hours. It is now down to about 35 hours per week not counting the part time workers. For everyone to have a "fulltime" job the work week has to come down further - 30/28/25? hours per week. This of course would raise the cost of products and services, but everyone would be working. Of course wages must be raised; a person cannot live on the minimum wage of $7.25 per hour. Unfortunately, I do not see economists thinking in these directions, and most certainly not the Congress (Maybe a slight improvement in the "Minimum Wage").

World Growth Limits

The previous several paragraphs relate primarily to the United States, maybe Western Europe, but not to most of the World's population. As can be seen from the data in Chapter 1, the population of the World has a long way to go to achieve the standard of living we enjoy in America or Europe. This driving force to improve the living standard in the developing nations will be a major influence on a continuing growth in the World GDP.

However, as previously noted, the Earth cannot support a population of 11 billion people, circa 2100, at the ultimate standard as set by the United States – a 300 **Q** per billion people. There is not enough land, water, or resources in the World for this level of economy. Hence the bottom line is that there must eventually be a status quo, a leveling out of GDP, only the supply of replacements, albeit more sophisticated products. Summing up in one word this last thought for the United States and to a lesser extent, later in time, the World – "Status Quo!". I have not read of a single social economist who has addressed this inevitable conclusion. They preach that more growth, a higher rate, is the obvious approach for the future. As a commentary, for two thousand years before the Industrial Revolution there was no growth – "Status Quo".

Many economists opinionate – A key to a better life is more education for all the people. Certainly universal, better, education is desirable. It would certainly increase the quality of an individual's life and might even bring a more logical influence to our governing bodies. However, it would not change the overall spectrum of jobs that are available and necessary for a nation to function. Higher education does improve the chances for an individual to achieve a higher standard of living, but it does not change the need for a spectrum of jobs from the lowest laborer to the most learned scientist. If everyone were a college graduate we would still need trash collectors, waiters, truck drivers, politicians, engineers, scientists, etc. There must eventually be a status quo, and the life of the low level worker must be acceptable. This leads us to a current United States and World issue of "Inequality", which is discussed in the following chapter.

31

Chapter 6

Inequality

There are several forms of inequality in the World. The principle one most often thought about is financial or economic inequality. This form inequality is the difference in income and wealth between the richest and poorest nations of the World or between the individuals in that nation. Therefore, this is both an issue and a concern to all of the nations/regions/people, from Africa the poorest region to United States the richest nation.

It is difficult to separate inequality from economics so in the following discussion there are clearly overlaps. In addition, as related to both of these is that of education. As education is of major importance to all nations, rich and poor, it will be discussed in the following chapter. Its relationship to both economics and inequality will be covered there.

There are several major forces that influence individual inequality and probably the most important are Race and Cultural background. In a country with multiple ethnic groups, such as the United States, it is obvious that white, European descendents, dominate the larger corporations, the State and National legislative bodies, and certainly the financial institutions. These kind of professions require a higher degree of education and in many cases wealth, but are these attributes due to being smarter, a higher Intelligence Quotient (IQ) or to the family circumstances. These kinds of questions have been considered forever with no final agreement – Are Whites smarter than Blacks? – Are Jews more intelligent than the rest of us? Although this question of intelligence, particularly for the individual, does bear on inequality as discussed in the chapter, I think it more directly relates to education, and therefore is more extensively discussed in the subsequent chapter.

Another significant inequality is that of the health in a nation. The poorest nations have little to no money for this to improve the status and even the richest sometimes do not do it too well. These issues will be reviewed subsequently in the chapter on Health.

Two Forms of Inequality

There are two forms of inequality that are generally a sub-heading under the broad category of economics, and are result of the mal-distribution of income or wealth. For example, the difference between the income of Blacks and Whites in many countries results in economic inequality, but this can also be considered to be racial inequality. Independent of economics, major differences in religious beliefs in a nation can also cause internal inequality. These are secondary effects so the following discussions deal primarily with economics per se.

Economic Inequality

A measure of a nations equality compared to other nations is the average annual income per person in that nation.

This income value parallels to a large degree the previously discussed Gross Domestic Product. A dollar per year income, circa 2012, for many nations – richer to poorer follows: .US/Canada $45,000; Western Europe $34,000; Japan $30,000; Russia $16,000; China $9,000; India $3,000; Sub-Sahara Africa $2,000. These numbers result in the fact that the richest nation's average individual has over 20 times the income of the poorest. Even with this spread, among the all nations there are poor, middle income, rich, and supper rich. This mal-distribution of both income and wealth has been around for a long time and has always been an issue, some times with violent consequences.

As noted, the income distribution in the prior paragraph listed only the "Average" values and therefore does not represent the consequences to the poorest, or the influence that high income brings to the rich and ultra rich. In all countries there is similar income spread, although in the richer nations there is more income and wealth in all levels of society, poor, middle. and higher middle income brackets.

This incredibly wide variation of individual income and wealth from the poor to the very rich is present in all nations but the distribution between the classes is different. This wide variation in a rich country can be illustrated by a tabulation of these data for the United States and it is only through these numbers that the magnitude of this issue can be understood.

For ease of comparison they are summarized in Table 5. A consistent set of these kinds of data are difficult to determine so this table can be view as rough estimate, but it does convey the right impression.

Table 5

United States Household Income and Wealth

	Income $/Year	Wealth Net Worth - $
The Lower 10%	2,000	-6,000
The Median 50%	50,000	80,000
The Top 1%	400,000	7,800,000
The Top 0.1%	7,000,000	30,600,000

The 30 million dollars in wealth of the 0.1% doesn't come close to the ultimate levels – Bill Gates at 79 billion dollars, and there are six other Americans among the top ten wealthiest of the World with over 40 billion in net worth.

Standard of Living

Another issue with this concentrated wealth in the United States is both the power it yields and the fraction of the capital it controls. For example, the top 1% control 39% of the capital investments while the lower 90% of the population have only 26%, and even this lower percent owned by the 90% is diffuse – not much influence. In terms of power, think about the United States Congress which is beholden to money to get elected, and after that there has been and continues to be modest (can not be prosecuted as illegal) quid pro quo. Wall Street, corporations, and the ultra rich control the laws and regulations to their benefit without too much concern for the lower classes.

Although dollars per year income is clearly a measure of how one lives it doesn't tell the whole story. A better measure is the "Standard of Living", however this is a function of a lot of conditions, housing, physical assets, well being – health and education, free time, and many more. Unfortunately, all of these contributions to a better life, a higher standard of living, can not be quantified by a number – they can be talked about and philosophically evaluated as being more or less important, for they are important.

To think about this relationship, it might be useful to consider how the standard of living has changed of the last 200 years. The starting point for the most dramatic improvements in the standard of living begins around the year 1870 – well into the industrial revolution. To consider the changes since that date requires a base point of what was available, or not available, to society both in and out of their home – if they were lucky enough to have one. Transportation for nearly all the people was walking, but the rich had horses or a carriage. Railroads were around, but they were mostly for commercial transport. Nearly all homes had no indoor water, none with running hot and cold, and sanitary problems were handled by an outhouse in the back. There was no central heating and even the poshest residences were lighted with candles or oil lamps – electric lights were still decades away. In that era the rich bought spermaceti whale oil candles, brighter, burned longer, but this oil was much more expensive.

In the next 60 years, 1870 – 1930, dramatic changes in the standard of living occurred in the United States, and to a somewhat lesser extent in Western Europe. The improvements in a home can be summarized by the five new "Connectivity" changes – Electricity, Running Water, Sewer Systems, Telephone, and Natural Gas. Central heating was a major change from the one room heated by a pot belly wood burning stove. The invention of the electric motor and the internal combustion engine brought street cars, automobiles, busses, and in the cities, subways, all changing how people can move – more than the mile or two walking.

Cities also had a dramatic change, they became more vertical. The electric elevator permitted buildings to have more that three or four floors raising the density of business and population. Subways tied it all together.

The next 40 years, 1930 -1970, a period of high productivity in the United States, continued to improve the standard of living for most Americans. More efficient manufacturing, with lower costs, brought the many new inventions to a large segment of the public. Most of these things are now in the modern home but it was in this time frame that they were introduced. The list is long but impressive: Washer/Dryers – replaced the wash board and hanging on a line; Refrigerators – replaced the ice box and the ice man delivering 25 or 50 pound block a few times a week, and more recently a Freezer: In the kitchen – mixers, coffee makers, garbage disposers, toasters; and entertainment, the radio was replaced by the television sets and you might consider the Cell Phone to be a form of entertainment.

The last 46 years, 1970 – 2016, has not had a continuation of the incredible number of earth changing inventions of the prior hundred years. This period has been more of a evolution or refinement of what was already here. The cell phone has pretty much replaced the land lines but it is still only communication, albeit more convenient. Automobiles don't go any faster, but they are safer, more comfortable, and if you want to pay for it more luxurious. Television sets are larger, flat screen, and better color, but their function has not changed. The internet is certainly new and extremely useful – I can not say the same for Face Book and Twitter but most of the public think they are great. From this brief list, it is clear that there is a high probability that few, if any, earth shaking inventions are likely to happen.

So in the United States where is the growth that most economists say is "Required" for a healthy or robust economy coming from. All the politicians say - "I will bring back the growth (and improve inequality)", but none of them have a clue as to how they will do it, or what changes have to be made. A Congress divided will not even seriously address the fact that the last 40 years, which have had a nominal but continued growth, has all gone to the upper 1% of the population.

These last paragraphs describe the developments in the United States and to the highly developed countries of the World, but not to the poorest nations which are still back in the year 1870. That may sound harsh but let me illustrate this statement with a few bits of data about how the poor of the World currently live, or maybe the correct word is survive. Over a billion people have inadequate access to water and a billion and a half people lack basic sanitation. Lack of clean water is a direct cause of nearly 2 million deaths a year from diarrhea alone. In Sub-Sahara Africa 80% of the people cook with biomass. More than 1.6 billion people, over 20% of the World, do not have electricity. Finally, over 8 million children die from poverty each year. All of this says that none of the incredible inventions and developments of the twentieth century are available to most of the poor of the World.

Riots and Uprisings

You might think that this gross inequality within a nation would cause civil uprisings, even a civil war. This does not seem to happen as we look at the past history. The earliest mention income inequality, or perhaps the poor being too poor, dates back to Roman times – One BC. However, civil wars of that time were more political and a struggle for power between them, albeit the poor were involved. Studies have shown that it is much easier to start a civil war or uprising from specific group, not a general distribution among many diverse people that comprise a broad segment called "Poor".

Riots and uprisings led by a smaller group have happened many times in most of the nations of the World. The group which sparks or leads such uprising nearly always has some bond which holds them together – cultural, ethnic, race, religion. It does not seem too likely that, even though the poor have a legitimate bitch (a crude word but I could not think of a more appropriate one) there will be no national revolts.

The closest event in the United States of recent vintage that was significant enough to be in the news for many weeks was "Occupy Wall Street" in 2011, was pretty much limited to New York City. This whole effort against the nearly criminal dealing on Wall Street, and the absence of reasonably good jobs, fizzled out for lack of a leader, money, or sufficient support from the hundreds of thousands that were affected. These were not only the poor, but many others that were hurt by Wall Street disaster. To be successful, or to accomplish some of the objectives of a depressed group, the group must be very large, have a specific agenda, and an incredibly powerful leader. The best, relatively recent, person who I believe demonstrated such capabilities was Dr. Martin Luther King.

Over the years, there have been many uprisings/riots that were related to the poor, and their inequality, but they, like Wall Street above, accomplished very little, and as can be seen from the data earlier in this chapter the poor are still very poor. There does not appear that there is any way out of this dilemma, but only a slow upward movement as the poorer nations increase their Gross Domestic Product with the hope that some will rub off on the more destitute and make their life more livable.

Upward Mobility

Upward mobility was mentioned in the prior chapter on Economics, but it is also a function of inequality, so it deserves a little more thought as this chapter closes. It was previously stated that there must eventually be a status quo, a distribution - low level jobs, service jobs, manufacturing, financial, scientific, political, topped off by the super rich, who may, or may not, work. Obviously this spectrum of work and occupations will have a wide distribution of income and wealth so that inequality is inevitable. Therefore, the issue is: Income must not be so dispersed toward the top that the lower jobs do not pay enough for a satisfying life. Where this line can be drawn is yet to be determined.

In the United States it is conceivable that Congress could pass laws /taxes that would help the poor. It is absolutely clear that the top 10%, 1%, 0.1% of the population do not have to get any richer. The "Trickle Down" theory, their money will help the poor, has been shown not to work. As previously noted, essentially all of the large increase in GDP over the past 40 years has gone to this top, already wealthy, group.

On the minimum wage law, at $7.25 an hour, a person could not survive even if they had two jobs. Recently there has been some movement in this area, particularly by the States and there is some talk in Washington. This lowest level wage may solely migrate upward.

Much of this last discussion has been for the United States but the same kind of thoughts can apply to the other industrial nations, and with some modification to the developing and poor nations. Clearly there is a need for change.

Chapter 7

Education

An issue that is always talked about when considering "Inequality" is **"Education" – reading, writing, mathematics.** It is true that in the poor and developing nations the population is mostly illiterate. About a billion people in the World cannot read or sign their name. Over 70 million kids of primary school age are not in school. This is the current status and it might be changing as more nations try to move toward an improved economy, but what comes first – the chicken or the egg?

What is the purpose of education? In my opinion, there are three principle components.

- To provide the knowledge to enter and be productive in the work force – this is sadly lacking in most educational systems

- To develop in people attributes that leads to a desirable social network, both within a nation and between nations of the World

- And for the individual, the ability to think logically and to evolve a fuller, happier life.

The idea of, "Think Logically", a prime objective of education, is difficult to teach – it is not a course that you can enroll in, ether in grade school or college. It can not be taught but must be learned. It is a combination of philosophy, science, mathematics, and may even be influenced by an understanding of history, both ancient and modern. To a large extent it develops from being inquisitive, seriously thinking about current and past events, their causes and consequences, and certainly from reading. Reading! - but what? Although it is a bit of an ego trip, it might be interesting to hear my views on a few of the hundreds of books I have read over the past 85 years.

I might first comment on the first bullet above. My college degree was in Chemical Engineering, but after my experience on the Manhattan Bomb Project in World War II, my introduction to nuclear engineering, I read many books on physics, nuclear technology, radiation etc. This changed my profession, so for all my working career I became a Nuclear Engineer, including being an Adjunct Professor at New York Poly-Technic University.

A Reading List

Back to my reading, as a kid I had a number of "Big Little Books" (These were fat, roughly an inch thick, and four inches square), a few novels, and for magazines, the National Geographic, Popular Mechanics, and Popular Photography. As an adult, after my technical books in college, the other books I enjoyed or worked through later in life, is large and varied. The following is an abbreviated list of some of those I both enjoyed, or struggled through – as they were considered important in the literature, so I thought I might learn something. Although I did not read them in this order I thought it better to list them in published chronological time.

- **Aesop's Fables** (600 BC) Although there are more than 600 anecdotal fables dealing primarily with conversations between two animals you may be familiar with only a few – "The Tortoise and the Hare", "The Ant and the Grasshopper" – They all deliver a philosophical, or a better way of life message.

- **Plato** (400 BC) His philosophy, people relationships, and quotes from the other contemporary philosopher - Socrates, who did not write any books that survived

- **Titus Lucretious** (75 BC) "The Nature of Things" – This epic poem is the only writing of this Roman not lost and is an amazingly modern view of "Things". He dismisses the Greek version of matter and talks of atoms and other physical earth phenomenon that were not even thought about until the late "Renaissance".

- **Dante Alighien** (1300 AD) "The Devine Comedy" First, "Comedy" at that time was not funny but more a narrative or a play. The book is a visual, graphical description of a soul's journey through the many layers of Hell and so moving and scary that church attendance went up significantly after it was written.

- **Immanuel Kant** (1775) "The Critique of Practical Reason" A major philosopher, he differed from others with his premise is that "Practical Reasoning" is the foundation of philosophy.

- **Herman Melville** (1851) "Moby Dick" The miserable living conditions, the life and death of seamen on a whaling ship of the time – a novel but realistic.

43

- **Charles Darwin** (1859) "The Origin of the Species" An incredible demonstration of an inquisitive mind as well as one of the first great books on the science of life.

- **Charles Dickens - Charlotte Bronte** (ca 1850) "Great Expectations"- "Jane Eyre"- Others - interesting tales of how life was in the 19th century for both the poor and the rich – more descriptive, and certainly more readable, than histories.

- **Samuel Clemens – a.k.a. Mark Twain** (1876) "Tom Sawyer" – "The Adventures of Huckleberry Finn" - Fiction, but a great history of rural life as seen by both black and white kids along a river.

- **H. G. Wells** (1890s) "War of the Worlds" – "The Time Machine" – "The Invisible Man" are only three of his many interesting, imaginative, and forward looking books. His view of people and how they act is penetrating.

- **James Joyce** (1920) "Ulysses" You can try this but it is one of the few books I gave up on after only 50 pages – however, it is considered a classic.

- **Jawaharlal Nehru** (1939) "Glimpses of World History" History does not have to be boring. Nehru wrote this book as a series of letters to his daughter while he was in prison – an amazing document composed without library references – incredibly brilliant and readable.

- **Anne Rand** (1943) "The Fountainhead" United States capitalism as it develops in the career of an extremely talented architect – a good story

- **H. Allen Smith** (1944) "Low Man on a Totem Pole" – With an introduction by Fred Allen - Smith, a journalist for the New York World-Telegram, writes clever, funny anecdotes about real people, but some with fictitious names for obvious reasons – a great read.

- **George Orwell** (1949) "Nineteen Eighty-Four" Orwell's view of an ultimate Police State, thirty years hence. It hasn't quite happened but in some ways it is getting close

- **Professor C. Northcote Parkinson** (1957) "Parkinson's Law" The Professor's clever, funny, and profound view of how businesses and Governments behave – e.g. On corporate finance committees – "...time spent on an item is inversely proportional to the sum ($) involved."

- **Herman Kahn** (1960) "On Thermonuclear War" A fearful book by a scientist on the possibilities of catastrophic nuclear war between large nations. He developed a scenario for 160,000,000 deaths and this was with the original fission bombs, not the later developed huge hydrogen weapons.

- **Rachel Carson** (1962) "The Silent Spring" - Not 100% scientifically accurate but gives a persuasive message and serious concern on the future of flora and fauna on the earth.

- **Dr. Edward U. Condon** (1969) "Scientific Study of Unidentified Flying Objects" This is the official Government summary of the UFO sightings to that date. It goes to great length to dismiss all sightings, and in the end they find that 7% are so well documented that they are still "Unidentifiable"– But, because we did "Identify" 93%, the remainder must be equally explainable – the implication being that they are not from outer space. Must reading for the UFO enthusiast.

- **J. K. Rowling** (1997-1999) "Harry Potter et al" There were seven, but read at least one just for fun.

- **Thomas Piketty** (2013) "The Rise and Fall of American Growth" This French economist develops a very detailed, and also interesting, analysis of nations economic growth from 1800 to the present. Not a prediction of the future, but his history indicates that exponential growth in the economy is not possible – hence a worry for the future.

- **Picture and Art Books** (1900 – 2016) This category is not exactly reading, more browsing, but these kinds of books should be in everyone's library. Photo books, like those great Western Scenes of Ansel Adams, or the sailing photographs by Morris Rosenfeld, are beautiful to look at and relaxing to the mind.

Rankings in the World

Back to education and how it stacks up in the World. Many agencies have ranked/rated the nations standing in education and the various ranking are all are in general agreement. However, they deal primarily with the developed, or developing, nations, not the poorest, and I have not been able to determine the procedures or tests that lead to the listings. To put some perspective on this issue, Table 6 lists a few of the nations to give a feeling as to how they rank – large to small, rich to poor. This listing by the Organization for Economic Co-operation and Development (OECD) is more complete than many as it rates three categories – Reading/ Math/ Science. These qualifying tests to determine these rankings were given to students, 15 year olds, in 2012, but this kind of rating does not change quickly. Other organizations have developed similar ratings and these are in generally good agreement.

Table 6

Education Ranking by Nations

Nation	Reading	Math	Science
Shanghai-China	1	1	1
Finland	3	3	2
Canada	4	5	6
Japan	6	6	3
Norway	9	15	19
Switzerland	12	4	11
United States	**15**	**26**	**18**
Germany	16	10	9
United Kingdom	21	24	12
Mexico	35	35	35

The nation ranking does not tell the whole story but numeric scores can give an indication of the specific level of education, not perfect, but better. Rather than go through another table a few comparisons tell the story. The top nation - Shanghai-China: Reading/Math/Science are 570/613/580. In the middle of the list – United States the score: 500/487/502. The lowest, not in the World, but on this listing – Mexico has a score of: 424/413/415.

Improvements?

The question of how to improve education has developed significant differences in approach among the "Experts". Everyone seems to agree that better teachers are needed and this would raise scores. The phrase - "Raise Scores" - is many times the basis or criteria for doing better, rather than increasing thinking, logic, and evolving an education useful for future employment. The philosophy seems to be – "Train students to take a test".

Better teachers or reading ratings do not necessarily correlate with money spent. For example: United States, at a reading rank of 15 has the highest cost for grades 1 to 12, a total of $15,000 per year per student. Finland, at ranking number 3 spends $10,000, and South Korea, number 2, only $6,000. China is out of this World at a reported $2,000.

Educational experts have studied these kinds of data and have never been able to come to agree on a policy for educational, training, that is "Best". The range has been wide – pre-school, more parental involvement, and of course to create in the student an interest, a desire, a motivation – But how? In the poorest regions of the World, Sub-Sahara Africa, it is generally agreed that practical training for future work, rather that the typical "ABCs" would be beneficial, maybe some numbers and simple arithmetic. In South Korea there seems to be a philosophy of teaching knowledge useful to practical applications in the outside World – in arithmetic, not a mathematical formula per se but calculating the volume of a box. The impressive education results in Korea might also be a consequence of the philosophical principles in the family to get ahead you must be educated. This paragraph may not be too precise or accurate as it is not an actual reporting of the words of the educators, but more my impressions from the reading I have done on the subject.

In the United States, because we are at ranking 15 and the "Educators" are concerned, but the recommendations on education policies are all over the map. The suggestions are endless: Pay teachers more; Smaller classes; Get federal Government out and put education in State hands (We would probably have 50 different approaches, may be 51 with the District of Columbia); More Charter schools; More parent involvement; More homework - Less homework; More science and math. The list could go on, but you have the idea – lots of suggestions but, in the past, not much progress.

Teach-ability vs Learn-ability

One of the questions always asked when it comes to the success, adequacy, or failure, of education relates to two major positions on "Teach-ability" or "Learn-ability". The first is the intelligence of the kid, and second is the environment that the kid lives in. There have been many studies to try and establish if there are inherent differences in the intelligence, IQ – Intelligence Quotient, between races, nationalities, or ethnic groups. Are the genes different, smart kids are born of smart parents, or do smart, rich, parents provide the environment to develop intelligent children. There is evidence on both sides of this argument.

There is a distribution of intelligence in all races and groups of people – a few of the people are extremely smart, most are around average, and some have a problem. This

49

spectrum of intelligence of a large group is mathematically distributed by what is called a "Bell Shaped Curve" – high, and relatively flat at the top (the average) and tapering off to zero at both edges – it does look like a bell. There was a best selling book, "The Bell Curve" – 1994, by Herrnstein and Murray which addresses in 800 pages – "Intelligence and Class Structure in American Life". It was very controversial as was thought to show that Blacks were less intelligent than Whites. The "Bell Curves" did show a shift to the left, the less intelligent end, but that leaves open the question as to whether this shift is a difference in genes or environment. It is absolutely clear that there would be such a shift due to environment, but does this account for the total shift?

The most prevalent view of this question, is that all races, ethnic groups, are born with equal intelligence, but there is evidence which shows otherwise. Counter to the prevalent opinion, there is nothing in biology to suggest that the brain does not follow Darwinian principles, in theory there can be differences. There is a broad, but not conclusive indication from nation testing that the Chinese and Japanese average IQ is a several points higher (104-105 vs 100) than other nations, but does not prove a gene theory – it still could be the environment or culture.

There is one ethnic group that demonstrates a very large, real difference in average intelligence and that is the Jewish segment of the Worlds population – only 0.2%. There may be several influences driving this shift: They try harder – Social pressure, "My son the Doctor/Lawyer...". Judaism stresses learning and a philosophy - That to survive as a small ethnic group, you must be literate. There is real evidence of higher intelligence is in a segment of the population descended from Ashkenazi Jews from the near east and Europe. Their average IQ test is 117, a huge shift upward that cannot be explained by anything but better genes. This brilliance is further documented by many facts. A Jewish scientist is 100 times more likely to receive a

Nobel Award. In the most elite universities, Yale, Harvard, Brown, and Columbia, even though they are only 2% of the population of America, they make up 28% of the student body. They also represent a similar fraction of the college professors. This evidence of higher intelligence is overwhelming in this group, so this does demonstrate that all people are not born with equal, the same, intelligence. However, environment and training do help.

Religion and Education

Around the World, and to some extent in the United States, the influence of religion in education can be modest to extreme. In the Mid-east, many/most Arab countries, religion is the school. With education being controlled 100% by the State there develops in the student not a logical and informed view of the World but the view the State wants to promote. I doubt that much can be done about this issue. There might be some hope through the World-Wide-Web, as this source of information may be useful in bringing out a different view of the other World countries, that is if it isn't censored too much.

Even in United States some religions have a serious problem with teaching the truth, particularly in science and evolution and geologic history. Darwinism, to use a single word, is recognized by all reputable scientists as both rational and representative of how animals, plants, trees – all living things evolved. Evangelical Christians believe that the Bible is the only truth and therefore refuse to teach Darwinism", or at best put it forward as a competitive theory in the science department vs "Creationism". They claim Creationism as a science without one iota of scientific evidence – and to add to the idiocy the World is only six thousand years old.

One other thought on higher level education in the United States is the fact that we a falling behind in developing the engineers, scientists, physicists, mathematicians that made America the most productive, inventive, and manufacturing capital of the World. Although the number of Doctoral graduates in science is staying reasonably high, it should be noted that over 40% of those degrees are going to foreign students. Another indication of our decline in science and engineering is the decreasing percent of those degrees as compared to other nations. In Japan, for example, their percentage of science and engineering degrees is 63%, in China, rapidly coming up in these fields, it is 56%, and in the United States the level is down to 35%.

Education, as shown by the World ratings, is not too healthy in the United States and there does not seem to be any useful or convincing plan to improve the situation. This failure seems to be worse in the science and engineering fields, which is unfortunate, because these disciplines are the road to the future.

Chapter 8

Health

The health of nations can be assessed, measured is too strong a word, in many ways. The broadest judgment is more philosophical, a personal opinion – "Is the nation healthy?" The medical experts have quantified this question with statistics. Among these statistics there are perhaps three numerical that are commonly used, and a fourth more judgmental. A new fifth is both worrisome and will be controversial.

- Longevity – What is life expectancy at birth?

- Birth Survival Rates

- Mortality Amenable to Health Care – Those lives which could/probably have been saved with adequate, better, health care

- Availability of Health Services – Health facilities and Doctors per capita

- Medical errors – Possibly a serious cause of death

There can be more, but noting how nations rate on these criteria give a reasonably good assessment of their health care system and based on that ranking - The issue a need for improvement.

The Industrial Nations

Numerical data are available for all of the industrial nations of the World. In the following tabulation I will select a only few of those nations to indicate how the United States rates in the World. You may be surprised.

Table 7

Mortality Rates of the World

	Longevity		Birth Survival	
	Rank	Years	Rank	Deaths/1000
Japan	1	84	1	2
Spain	2	83	8	3
France	9	82	11	3
United Kingdom	20	81	37	4
United States	**34**	**79**	**57**	**6**
China	68	75	103	12
Congo	190	49	212	115

In the above table, the United States ranks 34th in longevity and 57th in birth mortality, lowest of all industrial nations of the World and many other less developed nations. At the lowest levels of longevity, a huge step downward, are the poorest and least developed nations – the Republic of Congo is typical of this group.

Medical Efficacy

Another quantification of the efficacy of the medical system of a nation is the number of those deaths that would probably be saved with better availability, and accuracy of medical services. This usually is called "Mortality Amenable to Treatment" and is inherently not too precisely determinable – there is both analysis and judgment involved. Not withstanding this caveat it a useful system and these ratings are listed in Table 8.

Before I comment on Table 8, the last bullet above relates to, and probably overlaps, medical efficacy, namely – "Medical Errors". There was a study recently published in the British Medical Journal that estimated that 251,454 deaths in the United States were caused by medical errors. This incredible number would make this the third highest cause of medical death – just behind heart and cancer. The causes include diagnostic errors, failure to do needed tests, bad communication, and others. As this is a new study, there are no comparisons to other nations. On seeing this review, I could not help but think of the 1971 movie – "The Hospital" in which George C Scott fails to cope with the multiple death threatening events. May be this farce is not far wrong.

Back to Table 8 in which there are three parameters that, in theory, could have a bearing on the adequacy of a medical system: The Gross National Income (GNI) per person; The number of Doctors per 1000 people; The hospital beds per 1000 people. Surprisingly, as can be noted from the data tabulated, there is no obvious correlation between these factors and a health result.

Table 8

Medical Services Data

	Deaths*		GNI	Doctors	Hospital	Cost
	Rank	/100,000	Rank	$/1000	Beds/1000	$/year
France	1	59	25	38,000	3.3	6.4	4,100
Japan	4	66	24	38,000	2.3	13.7	3,700
Spain	10	70	32	32,000	4.9	3.1	-
Germany	16	81	15	44,000	3.9	8.2	4,800
U Kingdom	19	86	27	36,000	2.8	2.9	3,200
U States	**25**	**124**	**11**	**54,000**	**2.5**	**3.0**	**8,700**
Mexico	28	137	69	16,000	2.1	1.7	900.

* Mortality amenable to treatment – that is, lives that probably could have been saved with better medical services

As can be seen from this table, the United States has twice the cost per year for all medical services among industrial nations, and with poorer results as summarized in the first column and the longevity and birth data in Table 7. Yet doctors and hospital beds are roughly comparable, except Japan and Germany, so why is there this obviously poor performance?

The United States

This poor performance of the United States has been studied extensively by many organizations and experts, with no universal agreement – just a lot of ideas and theories.

In my view, after reviewing many of these analyses, the primary cause is that all of the other industrialized nations have universal free medical service. This results in several different ways that the health system can respond to the medical needs of the population:

- Everyone is covered, hence potentially serious illnesses do not fall in a crack of the uninsured

- No one hesitates to seek medical attention as there are no co-payments or the need for approval to visit "Expert" Doctors.

- On costs – There is no Corporate/ Entrepreneurial incentive to over expand, or extend the treatment

- On drugs – There is virtual monopoly among the large corporations with little to no regulation by the government of the United States

The issue of costs in the bullet above needs a few numbers to demonstrate why the United States numbers are so high. For example, if we consider treatment by an expensive machine, the European nations (OECD) have 12 MRIs per million people and treat 46 patients a year per 1000 people while the United States numbers are 26 and 91 respectively – You have to pay for these machines. This factor of two is typically repeated in many ways, e.g. number of days in the hospital for a given procedure - the overall cost of that procedure - the cost of a surgeon – and the list goes on. It finally ends up that the annual medical cost as shown in Table 8 with the United States at about $8,000/year and the other industrialized nations with universal health service average about $4,000.

There are other, self-inflicted, factors that certainly bare on our poorer longevity and health, and that is obesity.

and diet. Obesity is a major cause of the increase in both diabetes and heart problems, and both of these can lead to earlier deaths. Fast food and 24 ounce sodas are not only a cause of obesity but can also contribute to malnutrition and illnesses.

I have not discussed the health issues of the poorest, the have not, nations – Sub-Sahara Africa, South Eastern tribes, and others. I did note in Table 7 the Republic of Congo data which is at the bottom of the list. Longevity is down from the 80s to 49 years and birth mortality up from 2-5 per 1000 births to an incredible 115. The solution is of course money and an improved economy, which would bring more food, clean water and more services. With very few drugs, and only 0.1 doctors for 1000 people, as compared to 2-4 in industrialized nations the health consequences are obvious. Improvement will be slow at best.

Chapter 9

Global Warming

This is long chapter as Global Warming is an issue that will eventually affect everyone in the World, some disastrously, others some, and a few only a little. There has been, and will continue to be, an increase in air and sea temperature, a rise in the ocean level, and a not fully understood shift in climates and an even less known change in local weather. The main issue on which there is no doubt is: "Global warming is real" - 97% of the scientists of the World agree. The remaining 3%, many politicians, financially motivated energy companies, generally say; "We need more evidence", and "This is a grand conspiracy promoted by the scientists"- with no rationality as to why there would be a conspiracy.

The Evidence

- Air-Sea-Land temperatures have been going up since 1950. The whole World is becoming industrialized in this time frame, together with major increases in car transportation, energy use, etc. This major industrial growth releases more and more carbon dioxide (CO_2) to the Worlds atmosphere. This additional CO_2 in the atmosphere captures more of the suns energy raising the earth's temperature.

- This temperature rise varies throughout the World, but on average it is currently about 1.3 degrees Fahrenheit. This does not seem like much, considering the range of local weather conditions, but the rate of rise has been constant and continues upward. The artic regions have had a temperature rise much higher than the rest of the World – 3.6°F.

- Satellite images show glaciers to be melting.

- Satellite measurements confirm that this melting ice has raised ocean levels by 2.9 inches. If this past rate continued to 2100 the rise would be a little less than one foot.

- Sea ice (floating) is retreating in the artic such that there is an open northern passage from the Atlantic to the Pacific for commercial shipping for some months of the year.

- Nature has recognized the warming with tree budding out earlier and flowers blooming sooner.

- You can personally feel the difference – the last two years in the United States have been the warmest in recorded history. In the rest of the World, 15 of the last 16 years have been the highest in recorded history.

There is more detailed evidence, but these several bullets tell most of the story.

Carbon Dioxide – CO_2 and Methane – CH_4

There are actually two gasses that the nations of the World are releasing to the atmosphere which cause global warming. The gas usually talked about, Carbon Dioxide - CO_2, causes about 70% of the warming while the other large contributor is Methane, CH_4 - you know it as natural gas, causes the remaining 30 %. Showing a "Cause and Effect" is a key to proving a theory.

Scientific calculations have been developed which show that the extra suns energy absorbed by the CO_2 and CH_4 gas concentration in the atmosphere correlate perfectly with the measured rise in temperature. To give you another number, CO_2 in the atmosphere has risen from 300 parts per million (ppm) to a current level of 400 ppm, and going up at the rate of 2 ppm per year. There has always been CO_2 in the atmosphere, but the extra that man has added makes a difference to natures balance.

Although CO_2 is the gas most often discussed as the global warming issue, natural gas (Methane, CH_4) is important and may be less controllable in the future, so let me discuss that first. The concentration of CH_4 in the atmosphere is much less than CO_2, 1.75 parts per million vs 400 for CO_2, but natural gas is 30 times more efficient in absorbing sun energy, hence this smaller concentration results in 30% of warming.

The man made releases of methane come from three principal sources:

- Fossil fuel production – 33% mostly from natural gas wells, processing, distribution

- Livestock – 27% primarily from cows and cattle, but lambs, pigs, and chickens all contribute

61

- Land Fills – 16% from the decay of organic materials - food wastes are a large source

In addition to these man made releases, which are about 60% of the total current releases to the atmosphere, nature adds another 40%. This is mostly from decaying organics in wet lands. Not much can be done about this fraction, but there is a major concern for the future. Above the Artic Circle there are huge amounts of methane trapped in the permafrost and as the tundra thaws, with Global Warming, and becomes a soggy mess, the CH_4 will start to be released. There is concern and some scientists think this will cause such large additional releases that World temperature will rise much higher than is currently predicted. This methane release from the thawing ground has a characteristic, called "Positive Feed Back" - Temperature rise causes methane release and that releases raises the earth's temperature higher causing still more release – a vicious circle. At what rate? - How much? - When? - Are all real and yet to be determined.

When you think about the three bullets above you have to wonder, not only how these releases can be limited to their current level, and can they even be stopped from getting larger. On the first, fossil fuel production, as natural gas is replacing coal, and more wells are being drilled to supply the added demand, the likelihood of reduced release seems unlikely.

The World, in trying to emulate the United States standard of living, is likely to demand an increase production of beef and milk. Estimates indicate that meat production will double between now and 2050 and as livestock and farming currently produce 27% of man made releases this increase in meat production will raise the total methane release by 17%.

On land fill, it is not too likely that any new technology for garbage disposal will be significantly developed, so not much change in CH_4 release can be expected. Incineration of wastes could be possible but I'm not sure whether the CO_2 from burning would be better or worse to the environment.

All of this discussion suggests that any future reduction of man made CH_4 release is just about zero, and it seems likely that there will continue to be increases in the release rate and together with a potential of large increases from nature. This view says that to control Global Warming to a more reasonable level most of the control must come from CO_2 reduction.

Even more worry-some than this 60 year rise in CO_2 concentration is the fact that the rate of rise has been increasing every decade. In the most recent decade it has been 2 ppm per year. Even if it leveled off at this rate, not too likely, by 2050 the concentration would have risen to 470 ppm, and there would be more earth changes. These projections imply that if it were possible to completely stop the release of carbon dioxide into the atmosphere we would stop the warming trend. I have not seen a calculation of this hypothesis; however, with the extra CO_2 already added temperature would continue to rise until an equilibrium balance was achieved.

We have talked about a rise of 1.3°F to 3.6°F but the real issue is – What are the consequences of this Global Warming? There are broad answers to this question. It is obvious that there will be climate change. Already mentioned, sea level will continue to rise and this will have a drastic affect on the population of some nations, with less, but real affect on others. These are the two principle changes, but the issue is in the details.

First on climate change the consequences are not precisely known. Scientist have been struggling with extremely complicated atmospheric models using the most powerful computers and have come up with a lot of estimates - I won't call them guesses because they have worked extremely hard to try to arrive at a defensible conclusion.

History

Before we get into the details, at least the future estimates, I think it is interesting to review how we got here, and from that information - to where we might be going. The actual start of warming is about 1950, but the trend was initiated at the beginning of the 20th century. As a result of the incredible increase in fossil fuel use it might be called the "Energy Century". You could even argue that the trend, though not too important, began with the industrial revolution with energy use really taking off by 1850. This 19th century best be named the "Coal Century", all the new energy was from coal, and coal use went from essentially zero in 1800 to 75% of all energy by 1900, which was orders of magnitude more total energy than in 1900.

In the 20th century coal burning still increased for electrical power production, but the two other primary energy sources, petroleum and natural gas, and like coal in the 1800s, there use went from zero to the levels of today, and still rising. Transportation, home heating, and more recently the use of gas for electrical production are the cause. Table 7 summarizes this dramatic increase in energy use in this past century. As discussed in Chapter 1, the energy is summarized in Q values.

Table 9

Energy Use in the 20th Century

In 1900	World	US
Population – Millions	1,650	75
Energy – Q for the Year	40	10
Q per Billion People	24	130
In 1950		
Population - Millions	2,250	161
Energy – Q for the Year	95	33
Q per Billion People	37	205
In 2012		
Population – Millions	7,150	315
Energy – Q for the Year	524	95
Q per Billion People	73	301

Notes: $Q = 10^{15}$ BTU Variations in the **Q** per year result from different sources, particularly for the earlier years. Values tabulated are reasonably correct and differences are not significant for comparison purposes.

There are two problems that are identified in the above table. First the total energy is high and growing. Essentially all of this energy comes from the burning of fossil fuels with the associated release of CO_2 into the atmosphere. The current level of CO_2 is already too high as it has shown to be the direct cause of the global warming rise to date and continues higher every year. In the period from 1950 to 2012 the average increase in World energy consumption was 2.1% per year.

This 2.1% rate would be considered quite good as compared to the current rate of rise. From the most recent data, 2008 to 2012 World energy growth has been about 7% per year, incredibly high by comparison and the reason that this issue has finally started to get some World attention. The details of this increase are even more disturbing. Fossil fuels are not created equal in their release of CO_2 to the atmosphere, with the worst being coal, next petroleum, and the least, but still a major release, is natural gas. In roughly this same time frame, circa 2011, the yearly growth of 7% is divided between: Coal at 10% per year; Petroleum at 1%; Natural Gas at 5%. Coal is a disaster. The net result of these data is an average CO_2 increase in the atmospheric concentration of 4% a year – 2000 to 2012.

Before we go to the future, it would be both useful and interesting to understand how much energy we receive from the sun and how that will be changing. The current measurement of the sun's energy "intercepted" by the earth is 1.36 Kw/m², that's thousands of watts per square meter. In regard to this 1.36 Kw of energy, think of 10 – 100 watt old incandescent light bulbs and a square meter is a little larger than a square yard. That is a huge amount of energy but fortunately it all does not stay on earth – more on that later.

In the last four hundred thousand years the temperature of the earth has gone up and down, glacier periods to hot eras - 14 °F cooler to 7 °F warmer than our current temperature. The earth started a lot warmer. Four billion years ago when the earth was forming it has been estimated that the temperature was extremely hot – around 3,000 °F and its surface was molten. All of the space debris crashing on the surface of the newly forming earth creates a lot of heat. At this temperature, radiation, heat lost to space, was enormous so the earth cooled. On the order of two billion years ago it was finally cool enough for the beginnings of life. It is interesting to note, that at the birth of the earth the sun was 30% cooler than it is now, and currently the radiation from the sun is increasing. However, this "increase" has nothing to do with global warming as the radiation intercepted from the sun will increase from the current 1.36 Kw/m^2 to 2.0 Kw/m^2 – two billion years from now. Long before that time the earth would have lost all of its water and all life.

How is it that earth is so lucky to have the "right atmosphere and temperature"? In one sentence - it has the optimum mass (weight), the right distance from the sun, which fortunately has the right level of radiation. If we compare earth to our neighbor planets the importance of these three factors are obvious. Venus, about the same mass as earth, is too close to the sun resulting in twice the solar radiation and a temperature of 850 °F. Mars has only 20% of the mass of the earth and thus gravity is not strong enough to hold much of an atmosphere or water, and therefore the planet has no way to average out the daily swings in temperature. Even though Mars receives only half the radiation from the sun as earth the daily swings in temperature ranges from a warm 98 °F to extreme cold at minus 190 °F. Future astronauts are going to have a hard time

Consequences

Although environmental and atmospheric scientists cannot predict what is going to happen in specific areas of the World as the average temperature continues to rise, there are some broader consequences that are real:

- Climates will change and higher average temperature will move northward in the northern hemisphere

- Associated with the migrations of temperature rise northward, farm crops, as appropriate, will also move north, which in turn will shift communities. However, some of the farmers might be fortunate enough to stay – corn farms in Kansas may grow date trees or have pineapple fields.

- Related, and another major influence on farming, will be a change in precipitation, a possibility of drought or more rain – where and how much to be determined.

- Glaciers and mountain snows will melt with the continuing rise in sea level.

- Floating ice in the Artic will be gone, opening up the fabled northern sea route between the Atlantic and Pacific oceans.

- Rising sea levels will flood many low elevation sea-side cities and areas and will jeopardize many others in ocean storms.

- The temperature rise in the oceans will affect coral growth, fish migration, and other changes still unknown.

- Wildlife will migrate with the climate, but some changes may not be possible – e.g. polar bears do not survive without floating Artic ice.

- There will be more severe storms and heat waves – already a problem in many regions.

It might be interesting to think a bit longer and expand upon some of the above bullets. Precipitation, rain, snow, is a topic that is generally not fully understood. The most common comment on warming is that there will be more droughts – deserts in the World. Actually there will be more rain - its day follows night, but where is the question – Where? As the ocean temperatures increase, this must result in greater water evaporation into the atmosphere, and since this cannot go on forever the evaporated water must come down – rain. Although not too scientific, but based on logic, as the surface water in the warmer regions of the ocean rises by 2 to 3°F, currently shown on some maps, the vapor pressure would also rise by 7%. Whether this will cause the same 7% increase in total rainfall I will leave to the meteorological experts, but there is absolutely no doubt that precipitation will increase. Meteorologists have not yet been able to predict the locations for more rain or a new desert.

An increase in storm frequency and severity has generally been predicted as a consequence of global warming. The US storm "Sandy" which caused havoc and huge property damage on the east coast in 2011 has been blamed on global warming. This is certainly possible and there is some logical scientific rational, more surface energy in the ocean which can generate higher wind speeds, but this is not proof. Historically, there have been other equally bad storms, before any global warming, that have hit the east coast. A review of storm statistics over the last 40 years, do not show an increase in frequency, but there is indication of greater severity

Sea Level Rise

Ocean sea level rise will result in a potential serious problem to ultimate catastrophes. The serious problems have already been demonstrated by flooding in many storms in Bangladesh. Large numbers of families have had to abandon homes near the sea and move to not much higher ground inland. The future problems are so indeterminate because there is no consensus as how high the seas will rise. Different organizations make different assumptions: How high will global warming go: How much Greenland ice will melt, which flows directly into the ocean: Secondary affects might be assumed, like the Polar floating ice and snow are gone which changes the global heating rate – more sun radiation is absorbed because it is not reflected to space by the white snow. The result of all of these different assumption is a prediction for the sea level rise in 2100 from which there can be no conclusion. All the estimates by several organizations, experts, have predicted/ calculated ranges for 2100 which have the following spread - all are in feet: 0.5/2.0; 1.3/4.0; 2.5/4.0; 2.5/6.5. So the total spread from of all of these estimates is from 0.5 feet to 6.5 feet, not too helpful except to indicate - a "Problem" or a World "Catastrophe".

When you look at this wide spread of the sea level rise, 0.5 to 6.5 feet by 2100, you have to ask – "Do any of the "experts" know what they are doing?" – the answer is – "Sort of". The basic problem is that no one knows how successful the nations of the World will be in controlling, limiting or increasing the CO_2 release into the atmosphere - and obviously not the experts considering the spread of their calculations. However, taking the average rise from the above experts, it is still 2.25 feet – a disaster, but not as large as is possible. Think about some of the World consequences if the high end of the range happens. First, many of the large cities of the World are located on the oceans, or on rivers whose water level is determined by the ocean. Further, large segments of the population have homes right on the sea shore, or on the beaches of small islands. These desirable locations are beautiful when there is no storm or sea surge, and many of these homes are just a few feet above current water levels. Again, consider the consequences from the major storm "Sandy", with only a few inches of sea level rise.

A few cities in the World come to mind as being an obvious candidate to have major problems with a sea level rise, and disaster at the 6 foot flood level. Venice, many times a year has a foot or so of flooding in San Marco Square, so add 6 feet of water to that in a flood tide and the buildings, including the beautiful Saint Marks Basilica will not have much of a chance. Half of the Lido Island will disappear. In the United States Florida comes to mind - the Everglades, the Keys – a large fraction of these areas will be gone, and in a storm Miami has a problem. Also in the south, New Orleans is already below sea level – Can we build another 6 feet or more of levees to protect an isolated city.

Among the many nations of the World that are most in jeopardy I would include the Netherlands and of course Bangladesh. Like New Orleans, major regions of the Netherlands are at or below sea level and the decision to try and save these areas or abandon them is tough call. Bangladesh is even more of a disaster but the results are inevitable – 70% of the country is slightly over 3 feet above sea level, so the consequences of 6 feet rise in the ocean is obvious. These are but a few examples but are typical of issues to be solved by nearly all the nations of the World. Not getting to this maximum level of disaster is of incredible importance.

The other major consequences of global warming, climate change, heat waves, change in precipitation patterns cannot be marked to a specific location so the affect on the population cannot be explicitly determined. All that can be added is pretty general and much of this has been high lighted in the bullets above.

Awareness of the Problem

A few scientists started to have concern about the possibility of global warming in the mid twentieth century but it was only later in that century that more scientists and World nations began to take notice. One of the authors who high lighted global warming early was James Lovelock, a long time member of the British Royal Society. His first book on the subject, 1972, developed the concept of a self regulating, living earth named "GAIA", and how our industrial age has started to damage this sophisticate control system. His most recent book, "The Revenge of GAIA", presents an extremely worrisome prediction of the consequences of warming in the twenty first century – our current path. If you think my future scenario develops dire consequences to the World, you should read "The Revenge".

In 1997 the industrial nations of the World met to discuss the global warming, more explicitly, how to limit, minimize the cause – CO_2 release from fossil fuels. The result of this conference named the Kyoto Protocol and the industrial nations "agreed" to reduce CO_2 release from the 1990 levels by 8% by the time frame of 2008-2012. Even this was a little bit of a game. England had already come down substantially from 1990 by the replacement of coal electric plants with natural gas. Further, from the World standpoint, even if they achieved the goal, which they did not, it would have made negligible difference as all of the developing nations, the fastest growing, China, India, Mexico, etc. were exempt from the agreement. This "Treaty" had no enforcing rules or conditions around it so it was more optics, a "Loss of Face" than anything else. United States - Clinton /Gore signed the agreement but it was never valid as the US Congress must approve all treaties, and its ratification was never pushed by either Clinton of Bush administration.

More nations of the World are now worrying, planning, proposing agreements to deal with, mitigate, may be even solve the issue of global warming. It has been quite a while from the Kyoto Protocol in 1997, to the "United Nations Climate Change" conference in Paris – November 30 to December 12, 2015, which was attended by 195 nations of the World. Prior to this meeting, a 146 nation committee recommended that the World try to limit the temperature rise to 5°F by 2100. The UN conference lowered that goal to 3.6°F, which has been calculated to require a 40% reduction in the release of CO_2 by 2030. There was "pie in the sky" talk of a 2.7°F rise which would require the CO_2 release to be down to zero in the time frame of 2030 to 2050. I think this number was developed to show where we are now as it is obviously impossible – back to the stone age.

Sources of Warming Gasses

In order to assess the possibility of achieving this 40% reduction in CO_2 releases it is necessary to examine where the CO_2 comes from – more details that coal, oil, and gas. Depending on who does the additions there are differences but the following are typical estimates.

- Electricity – 33% Typically, about 70% or more of electrical generation comes from fossil fuels with the lion's share being coal

- Transportation – 28% This is predominately road traffic at 85%, followed by aviation growing at 8%, marine use at 4%, and rail at only 2%

- Industrial – 20% This category covers an incredible range of products with cement manufacturing being the top, followed by steel

- Residential /Commercial – 11% This CO_2 release is nearly all natural gas with very little chance for significant change.

- Farming – 8% A sort of a combination of the above

Look at the above bullets and begin to consider how CO_2 releases can be cut by 40% by 2030, only 14 years from now. "Electricity" and "Transportation", the two largest CO_2 emitters, at 61% are where the reduction must come from. In the three remaining categories there is not much likelihood of any major reduction.

In the transportation sector, marine use is sacrosanct and for aviation use, except for some minor improvements in efficiency there cannot be much of an improvement. The number of flights can probably not be touched – historically there has always been more. That leaves the balance of the transportation sector. Fuel use in trucks has always been a concern of owners, as there is competition to be cheaper and to have higher profitability - so again not much a reduction can be expected. Finally, it comes down to private automobiles.

Mitigation

There are several possibilities to reduce fuel consumption in privately owned cars:

- Cars can be smaller, lighter, more efficient, lower horsepower – less fuel consumption

- More Hybrid and Electric Cars – They cost more and where does the electrical energy for battery charging come from?

- Fewer miles – More buses, trains, trams (street cars), all having significant lower fuel consumption per passenger mile.

On the first bullet, this has been, and continues to be, the car buying philosophy in Europe and in the Asian

Countries. As a result, European fuel mileage is on the order of 45 miles per gallon. This compares to the United States at about 32 mpg, or lower. This difference, if it were implemented in the United States would reduce fuel consumption for this sector by one-third. However, if you look at what is selling in the US its trucks, vans, and more power – check the TV commercials.

Some of this US trend toward power and size is a result of the current, very low fuel cost - the lowest in years. Not only do these lower cost influence purchases, but they also have some influence as to how many miles a person drives a year. As the cost of gasoline has gone down, annual mileage has gone up. This suggests that a tax on fuel would also be a step toward reducing CO_2 emissions. Such a tax on all carbon fuels, coal, oil, and natural gas, would also be an influence to lower consumption. There would not only be a direct affect – lowering the thermostat temperature in the winter, but a tax would also save energy by influencing improvements in better home and commercial building insulation. Manufacturers would also be more careful, and strive for higher efficiency in fuel consumption. The degree of energy savings is dependent on the level of the tax, and the argument used against such a rise is that it would raise the cost of living. Even though it would be useful – don't hold your breath.

After this aside on tax, let me get back to car mileage. President Obama's announcement that we will improve our fuel mileage for newly manufactured cars from the current level to 54.5 mpg by 2025 is certainly ambitious, and in my opinion unlikely.

The details of how to implement this significant change are still to be worked out and are yet to be demonstrated. It should be noted that trucks would not be affected by this order and they make up a transportation sector that has a high CO_2 emission rate. As transportation fuel use results

Robert William Kupp

in 24% of our total CO_2 emission, the proposed automobile MPG reduction would lower the total transportation sector by about 40%. This would be quite impressive. It should be noted however, that a change in new car mileage does not immediately transfer to the overall country – there are still many older cars on the road, so the transition is gradual and would not be fully implemented until more than a decade later. However, to get to the UN Conference objectives of a 40% total reduction, most of most of the balance has to come from electrical generation.

Electric Power

The major key for a successful CO_2 reduction effort must come from the electrical power industry, which releases 40% of the greenhouse gases. In the World 70% of this generation is from fossil fuels and most of this energy is from coal, the worst of the fuels. In the United States electrical power generation is similar at 67% from all fossil fuels and with 60% being coal. The balance is natural gas and just a little oil. The use of fossil fuels for power generation does not have to be the case. For example, France generates all of its electrical power requirements with only 10% of the power plants using fossil fuels, and nearly all of its power, 80%, comes from nuclear power stations with no CO_2 release. This demonstrates how nuclear power has been and can be a major factor in reducing global warming emissions.

This current status of energy in France introduces only one of the several technologies that are now being used, proposed, and developed to mitigate and lower emissions. Those "New" technologies most talked about are wind and solar power. It might be useful to consider what a future mix of these three technologies could be.

I've not mention another renewable that has been important in World electrical power generation – hydro power. This is certainly among the best of renewable power and has been successfully and economically demonstrated in thousands of power dams throughout the World. Unfortunately, because this is such a good source of energy, most of the useful river locations have already been developed. There are more, mostly for smaller, previously not economic locations, and a few more remote locations and these will certainly help with non polluting power needs of the future.

Both wind and solar power have been extensively talked about as the panacea to solve the future electrical requirements. In the past decade they have started to have some contribution but it is still very small – less than 1% in the United States and even less in the World. As costs are coming down with greater production volumes, their rate of introduction has been increasing. However, there is a limit to the fraction of electricity that can be generated from these renewable sources.

Sun power is only available for significantly less than half time, although in some regions on the earth it shines much of the time during the day. Unfortunately, these regions are not near New York, London, Paris and most large metropolises. For optimum use of solar energy new transmission systems are needed and with our current technology this new infrastructure is very expensive.

Another added cost for both solar and wind power is the need for an instant back up system when the sun goes under a cloud or the wind stops blowing. Basically this backup system must be a duplicate of the solar/wind generating capacity and would probably be natural gas generation, as this is the least costly plant to build. Think of this statement - with solar/wind, twice the generating capacity needs to be built and paid for. Also natural gas, the back up would add more CO_2, so sun and wind are not the perfect solution - Enter nuclear power.

Nuclear Fission Power

The biggest obstacle to nuclear power is the extreme anti attitude of the public – no one wants a nuclear power plant in their back yard, or evening their country - and for the most dedicated antis – any where in the World. As a retired nuclear engineer I must orate for several pages – if you do not wish to be brain washed, skip to the next chapter.

First on positive non-controversial facts - nuclear power is a fully demonstrated technology that in the past 60 years has been shown to be economic, releases no CO_2, and has demonstrated that it can supply a large fraction of a nation's electrical needs in a relatively short period of time. United States went from zero to 20% of our electrical demand in less than 50 years and France went to 80% in about 40 years. There are 100 operating plants in the US and in 31 countries of the World 440 plants generate 11% of the Worlds total electrical power. Currently around the World, 65 nuclear power plants are under construction.

The strong anti-nuclear view of the public is based on two perceived problems: The potential for a catastrophic accident and the future dangers of long term nuclear waste disposal. A more complete understanding of these issues, rather than the disaster oriented, scare tactics, promoted by the popular press and the media, may help to give a more balanced perspective to the reader.

The scare word that is always used is "Radiation" – it cannot be seen, felt, or detected without instruments, and it can be deadly. "Deadly" is the word always remembered as the human toll of Hiroshima and Nagasaki is remembered. Most radiation is quite benign and every person in the

World is exposed to radiation every day – from the sky, from the earth, from the home we live in, and periodically much more from medical diagnostics. To understand "Radiation" you must think in numbers, a new unit is the "Roentgen" or a small fraction - "milli-Roentgen", named for the man who discovered X-rays. Subsequently its definition was made more precise and the name changed to "milli-Rem" (mR). The average person on earth receives 360 mR per year from the above natural sources.

Radiation, since its discovery, has been shown to cause cancer - Roentgen's hand for example, or Madame Curie's death. The daily dose to all people, 360 mR, is too small a dose to determine a cause and effect. To try and estimate lethal effects of small doses an ultra conservative logic has been used. It is a little bit irrational but you might find the method interesting.

It has been determined that a radiation dose of 500,000 mR over a short period of time, and without medical treatment, is lethal to half the people. It is also known that 25,000 – 50,000 mR results in measurable biological effect, a reduction in white blood cells. Because 500,000 mR causes death it is assumed that one mR has a lethality of 1/500,000th – this is called the linear theory. From this theory, if 500,000 people each received one mR of radiation one would die. If we applied this same logic to aspirin the result become obvious and ridiculous. Chug-a-lug 100 aspirins and you die, hence one aspirin has 1/100th of lethality. If 100 people take one aspirin one will die – so much for the logic of linear theory.

Unfortunately, this linear theory is used in all safety analyses, and nuclear accident consequences. This results in a significant number of theoretical deaths from even a very minor radiation release if that low radiation dose reaches a lot of people. It automatically creates the impression – radiation, even a little is disastrous and that is what people remember when it is reported by the media.

Nuclear Accidents

In the past 60 years there have been two very serious nuclear accidents, Chernobly, Russia in 1986, and Fukushima, Japan in 2011. There were two other reactor accidents, minor from a radiation to people view, Windscale, England in 1957 and Three Mile Island, United States in 1979. Only the Chernobly accident resulted in immediate radiation deaths so I will briefly review that insane historical event.

First some background on safety requirements, both for design and for operation. Government approval is required before any nuclear power plant is given the license to build. As part of that licensing review a spectrum of theoretical accidents, their probability and consequences must be developed. As an aside, no other industry is required to do such an analysis. The ultimate accident in this series is given the name – "Maximum Credible Accident". In all of these theoretical events the consequences must be small for probable accidents and extremely unlikely – one in a million years for the "Maximum". Chernobly was an accident beyond this "Maximum". Independent of the "criminal" action of the plant operators this reactor design could not have been built any where in the World except Russia – it did not meet World safety standards.

The accident was a direct result on an experimental test that the local plant management decided run to test the reactor under very unusual conditions. However, to run this test three reactor safety systems had to be locked out that would have safely shut the reactor down. There was no Russian government review of this test by knowledgeable nuclear engineers. When the test was run, 1:23 AM, - March 26,

1986, the power in the reactor rose so rapidly that the reactor exploded destroying the building and spreading much of the extremely radioactive reactor core around the countryside. The overheated portion of the uranium core that was left in the reactor building burned for over two days. Helicopters dropping sand (water causes uranium to burn more) finally put it out, with a significant radiation dose to the low flying pilots.

In the few weeks after the accident direct deaths due to radiation, primarily to plant operators of the plant were only 13. Using the previously discussed "Linear Theory" and published radiation doses I calculated that there might be 2,000 addition deaths and the most pessimistic number I have seen is 9.000. The higher doses were to those workers who partially cleaned up the extremely high radioactive debris surrounding the plant. People still do not live in these contaminated areas but surveys of the returning wild animals show very little residual affect.

The most recent nuclear disaster was at the six reactor site, Fukushima on the Pacific coast of Japan in 2011. This accident was the direct result of one of the largest earthquakes ever recorded, greater that 8.9 on the Richter scale. As it was off shore it generated a huge tsunami wave flooding the electrical and emergency generator portions of the nuclear plant. Without this emergency power to cool the residual heat in the reactor, it was shut down immediately, the core underwent a melt down causing the subsequent release of radioactivity to the surrounding environment.

In the safety analysis of this site prior to construction, the possibility of a tsunami was considered and the prior 200 years of history at this site was evaluated. It was concluded that the plant should be safe against a 30 foot high wave, and a 33 foot barrier wall was built. Unfortunately, this tsunami was 43 feet high.

There was warning of the react core melt down so there was an evacuation of the area and the radiation dose to the public was quite small. It has been estimated that there might be a one percent increase in some cancers – not enough to be statistically detectable, except possibly for non-lethal thyroid cancer. There were 1,000 deaths resulting from the evacuation but no radiation deaths. The tsunami wave, which traveled up to 6 miles inland causing massive damage, killed 16,000 people.

The major United States nuclear accident was Three Mile Island. The reactor plant had to be decommissioned, a long and expensive task, but the radiation dose to the public was negligible. There was essentially no radioactivity released from the containment system – the large cylindrical domed concrete building worked just like it should. The cause was a complicated series of events, but finally topped off by miss interpretation of some of the instruments. In a sentence – cooling water which was available was not pumped into the shutdown core of the reactor in time – it partially melted.

That's it – 60 years since the start of the first plant, 440 plants later and 13 known radiation deaths and only the possibility of a few thousand more in the future – an outstanding safety record. Over the same period of time consider the consequences of health effects by the coal fired electrical generating stations. I do not have a total for 60 years but just one year of data will give you the picture. In the United States it has been estimated that there were 10,000 premature deaths from coal plant emissions in 2010. In the World, a recent, one year, total was estimated at 210,000 deaths and over 2 million serious illnesses – asthma, heart, lung, etc. The 60 year total – a few thousand possible nuclear deaths compared to tens of millions coal deaths, not even a contest. It is clear that by any standard nuclear power is safe and the more nuclear plants that are built the safer the World will be for as coal fueled plant are retired there will be no health damaging pollutants and of course no CO_2 emissions. Nuclear power should be the major contributor to limiting global warming.

In the opening discussion of nuclear power, I indicate that the other public concern is that of the difficulties of the disposal of high level nuclear wastes. This is primarily the uranium fuel with the contained fission products (the radioactive elements that are the result of fission) after three to four years of producing energy in the operating reactor. These fission products will remain radioactive for many tens of thousands of years - always becoming less radioactive, but it takes time.

Fortunately, the volume of these wastes is very small and therefore a lot of money can be spent to dispose of them safely. The key word here is "Safely", and for the nuclear energy industry, "Safely" is just about zero risk of anything potentially dangerous. Therefore, politically, nothing gets approved, no matter what the scientific evidence. An underground disposal designed and partially built was calculated to be safe for 100,000 years - it now has to be a million years. I could go on for quite a while on the scientific bases for disposal systems but I do not think this is the spot – it needs another book. Again, like the anti nuclear power view by the public there is a similar, not based on evidence, an equally negative view of nuclear waste disposal.

Nuclear Fusion Power

As indicated in the beginning discussion of nuclear power, the two big concerns by the public are a catastrophic meltdown accident and nuclear waste disposal. In comes the savior, "Fusion Energy" – No meltdown: Minimal radioactive wastes; No environmental gas release; Infinite power for the future. What more could you possibly want?

Unfortunately, Fusion Power is not here yet, and the question is – "Will it ever be?".

My first assessment of fusion was in a technical paper for the United Nations Conference on Atomic Energy -1955. This was a very optimistic view on the economics of a fusion power plant if it were successfully developed – only several times the cost of a current nuclear plant. A second fusion paper was a much more of an assessment dealing with the engineering problems in a fusion plant design and it was presented in the Second United Nations Conference held in Geneva -1958. I will get back to this paper after the technology and "Progress" of a fusion power plant is discussed.

Fission power, the 400 nuclear plants now operating, is the result of the splitting apart of a Uranium, or Plutonium, atom with the release of a huge amount of energy. The split-apart fission products, two new elements, are extremely radioactive. Fusion is just the opposite, two isotopes of Hydrogen atoms are bonded together, "Fused" - again with a large release of energy, but negligible radioactivity remaining. This is how the sun generates its immense power. However, for this fusion to take place require ultra high temperatures, a few hundred million degrees, and extremely high pressure – difficult to achieve and close to impossible to achieve together.

Serious scientific and engineering work started at the time of the first UN Conference, and the Chairman, Dr. Homi Bhabha, of the conference was asked: "How long before a working fusion power plant?" - "About 30 years!". He was asked the same question three years later at the second Conference, and thinking for just a second or two – "27 years!".

We are now 58 years later, with the World having spent hundreds of millions of dollars per year on fusion Research and Development, and the question still is – "How Long to a first demonstration fusion power plant?" - We have increased the time only a little bit – "40 years!" This is a statement from the inter-national team managing the current, $16 billion and rising, experimental fusion reactor being built at Cadarache, France – a small town near Aix-en-Provence.

This is called the ITER Project and is very large version of the prior designs called "Tokamak". The original Tokamak was built at Princeton University and it did produce a fusion reaction for a few tenths of a second. The principle of a Tokamak design is to compress together a plasma (that's atoms without their electrons) of hydrogen isotopes with an extremely powerful magnetic force, which also raises their temperature to over 100 million plus degrees – and fusion. This magnetic force is very unstable and the hydrogen plasma tends to fly apart.

However, fusion is a long way from electrical power. In the fusion process essentially all of the energy is in the release of neutrons (neutrally charged particles – part of all atoms) traveling incredibly fast, not the speed of light but fast. This speed has to be turned into heat energy, and when you stop a traveling mass heat is produced. It is like stopping a fast moving car – the brakes get hot. These fast neutrons are captured in a flowing liquid metal which heats up and flows to a heat exchanger to boil water into steam which turns a turbine to produce electrical power. I have just described a fusion power plant - not a Tokamak or ITER. These scientific experimental machines only deal with the first step – fusion alone.

We needed all this engineering talk to be able to understand why I believe that fusion power will never, maybe that's too strong a word, be developed to save the World. The basic difficulty is that the fast neutrons create a lot of problems.

85

First - The neutrons travel so fast that they act like a sand blaster on the wall of the huge vacuum chamber that contains the plasma, chipping out atoms from the surface. No one currently has a clue as to how long the wall will last. Further the blasting off of the wall atoms may, depending upon the rate, interferes with the plasma control.

Second – A significant number of the neutrons are not absorbed in the hot liquid metal, but are captured by the wall material, the huge cryogenically cooled magnets and their insulation, as well as all other components of this incredibly complex system. It isn't the loss of these neutrons that is important but when neutrons are captured in the nucleus of an atom it may turn that atom into a different element. In many cases that new element is radioactive and this will cause this whole complicated system to be deadly to humans. This would not mater when the plant is running normally. When shutdown from a failure of some component, and there will be failure in such a complex system, the failure cannot be repaired because a maintenance man cannot get near it.

Third – The cryogenic magnets which are made up of carefully managed metallurgy may be damaged by the fast neutrons – yet to be determined. Failure of even one of these multiple magnets would be a disaster. When a failure of similar magnets occurred at the Haldron Collider near Geneva it was out of service for about a year – and this was with full access by the engineers and repair staff needed to assesses and repair the damages.

This is clearly a negative view on the future of fusion, but even the ITER project, needed to make progress toward a fusion power plant, is in jeopardy. Since its inception the estimated cost to completion has gone up by a factor of three, its completion delayed by about ten years, and the sponsors, the European Union and seven other nations including the United States are debating future financing, as there is no firm final price. Maybe it is not possible to manage an incredibly complicated project with twenty nations trying to agree on all of the innumerable decisions.

Future Energy

Back to wind and solar power, the electrical generation system every one loves. World wide and in the United States these are currently a very small fraction of total electric power generated - 1% of the power in the World and even less in the US. A few nations that started early, primarily wind power, are Denmark currently at an amazing 39% and the United Kingdom at 15%. These percentages are all "Capacity" not energy "Generation". Both of these nations have great winds on their shores and the sea sore is not far from the user cities. Both of these factors contribute to these high numbers.

On a point made earlier both these sources are intermittent hence the installed capacity, maximum generation when the sun is out bright and the wind is blowing, can be a long way from the actual energy generated. A number reported for World solar power listed a capacity factor of only 11%, and the other necessary 89% of backup power is supplied by fossil fuel. At this kind of a capacity factor it would be difficult to justify building many more.

In order to make any major progress in reducing the rate of global warming, specifically cutting CO_2 releases to the atmosphere, requires money, and lots of it - first to build the generating stations needed to replace all coal plants, mostly nuclear and then for the infrastructure to optimize wind and solar generation, or bring power from more distant hydro-electric dams.

The next decade or two will determine whether the nations of the World leaders/politicians have both the power and the gumption to go forward. Will the people of those nations tolerate spending money on an issue that does not seem to affect me today but will "probably" be important/critical/absolutely necessary for the benefit of my children and grand children? That is a tough judgment to make, for historically, most of the nations of the World have been driven by near term economics – a laissez faire approach.

Finally, a final comment needs to be made on the developing nations energy future. China to some extent, but India and Sub-Sahara Africa are all trying to increase their Gross Domestic Product, and in so doing they will require more energy – electrical, transportation, manufacturing. India, and certainly Africa, do not have a lot of capita for investment, so their approach to that future will tend toward the least expensive route – coal for electricity, oil for transportation and gas for manufacturing, all releasing CO_2. I find it impossible to see how such development in these nations is possible without significant CO_2 release.

The World is going to have a tough time achieving even the modest, but ambitious, goals of the United Nations Paris Conference on Global Warming. Let us hope that the Multi-Nation proposed reduction in warming gases is successful and will not have too much of an effect on the developing nations – it is a difficult compromise.

Chapter 10

Terrorism

Terrorism is an issue, a concern, a happening, in just about all nations of the World. In the mid-east, the Arab countries and Israel, a terrorist act happens just about every day. It seems to be normal, a few deaths a day, and a hundred or so several times a month. Fortunately, in the United States a major terrorist event of more than a few deaths has occurred only rarely. However, everyone has a vivid memory, which induces great fear and anxiety - September 11, 2001 when 3,000 people died.

History and Status

This brief review of terrorist events needs some documentation. It is absolutely true that terrorism kills a large number of people through out the World. Since 2000 there have been 140,000 deaths due to terrorist attacks. There may be many more as it is difficult to separate terrorism from civil war. The nations of the World have been ranked from 1 to 10 based on the number of events, deaths and injuries. The nations rank: Iraq 10 - Afghanistan 9 - Pakistan 9 - India 8 and skipping a few Israel 6. The United States and European nations are all in the 4-5 range, and among the top 50, none are lower than 4.

However, United States has the record, as 9/11 was the largest single attack in terrorism history. Since that date the total deaths in America have been averaging 34 per year – a total of just over 400 since 9/11. Most of these are just a few deaths per event, but we tend to remember the more serious attacks. The most recent terrorist event being San Bernardino, March 12, 2015, in which the two terrorist killed 16 people. Before that the Boston Marathon attack only killed 3, but it is remembered because of the event and dramatic television coverage. Just a few months earlier, December 14, 2012 the Newton School attack killed 28.

Quite different from World Tower catastrophe, all of the attacks since have been by only one or two individuals. First, this tends to limit the scope and severity of any attack, but it also makes it extremely difficult to detect and prevent the event. Unfortunately, with the automatic weapons available, one or two people can cause many deaths - we have been very fortunate to date.

There is a new technology that would be available to a s small group, or even to a talented individual. Drones are becoming more and more common and the current concern is flying near airports. Certainly a worry, but a small drone would probably not bring down a jet – they just do not have enough mass. However, larger ones could be modified to carry a small to medium size bomb and this could be flown into a packed stadium, or Time's Square on New Years Eve. To date there does not seem to be a plan or a technology to prevent such an attack.

To pull off a complicated attack like 9/11 required much planning, money, and training. Four pilots were needed to fly the commercial jets. The planes had to takeoff at about the same time, and be fueled for a long flight - the energy from the fuel was needed to make a simple crash, which would not have collapsed a building, into an ultimate disaster. Because the planning and training for this event took so long and involved so many terrorists we can hope that today the Government will be able to detect and prevent a recurrence in time.

As noted above, to detect and prevent an attack by one or two careful terrorist is nearly an impossible job for the several government agencies. Trying to identify and provide surveillance on the many thousands of potential terrorist would require an organization many times the size of the FBI. It could also require a further infringement on privacy and human rights that a large fraction of the public would object to. One of the better chances for detection would be the reporting of unusual, questionable, activity of by a neighbor or from an acquaintance - not terrorism inclined.

The Risk of Terrorism

The more fundamental question on terrorism in the United States is why it is a top priority in the minds and concerns of most people – ahead of all other risks of death that we take for granted every day. Think about these risks and how they compare –

- Terrorism - About 30 deaths per year as noted above

- Automobiles – 34,000 deaths per year and a large fraction of these could be prevented using currently available technology – no cell phone connection while the car is moving

- Guns –10,000 homicide, 20,000 suicide - deaths per year

91

- Falls – 26,000 deaths, with most of these inevitable

- Accidental – 130,000 deaths

Think about this last bullet - accidental death. You are not very likely to be unlucky as the odds are pretty good – only one chance in 2,500. The odds on being a terrorist victim are 4,000 times less – in other words a chance of 30 deaths in 330 million people, or about one chance in 10 million. Not bad - so why the paranoia?

I cannot leave "Terrorism" with out mentioning one incredible and dangerous future possibility. It is not inconceivable that a foreign terrorist organization, ISIS, could steal an atom bomb from one of the nuclear nations – Pakistan or India, or could acquire one from North Korea. This scenario is not too likely but not inconceivable. Delivery to a United States harbor by a small boat or in a plane from one of the near islands could be managed. It is a lot simpler than the 9/11 scenario. Deaths would be millions or more.

Let us hope that the government surveillance, and cooperation from observing citizens, will prevent any catastrophic event and that we can live with the minor events of the past decade. Other nations survive and conduct relatively normal activities with orders of magnitude greater risks.

Chapter 11

Religion

It seems a bit strange to have an "Issue" on a category of every day life - "Religion", a philosophy of living that should be personal and have little influence on any one but you and your own family – a personal belief. Unfortunately, that isn't the way many religions are practiced around the World, so it does become an "Issue".

Religion, or a worshiping of a "God", has been around just about forever. The first written record of such worshiping was by the Egyptians in 4000 BC. Of course they were among the first to write anything. But there are many indication of prehistoric worship, carved idols and ritual sacrifices. The philosophers have considered this early phenomenon and have come to an opinion, not unanimous, that this worshiping of a god or idol philosophy would help with the hunting and gathering and prevent violence between individuals. Is this the first idea of "Brotherly Love", or are the paleontologist just dreaming. There is some indication that murder was a major cause of death in the age of prehistoric man. This is an interesting thought but it is based on slim evidence and not necessarily true.

Getting to more modern times, and a little history - When did the religions of the World originate? How have they survived? How have they changed? and most important – What is their philosophy and their objective? These all are a few of the key questions to the understanding of religion today.

Origins

First on their origins, and a very brief comment on their charter or characteristics

- Hinduism 3000 BC - Worship of one God, Animals are sacred, a Caste system, a relatively negative view of women

- Judaism 2000 BC - A single, all powerful God, as developed in the Torah, essentially the Christian Old Testament and by the prophet Abraham with a belief in the after-life

- Buddhism 480 BC - Not quite a religion in the classic sense having no God, but more of a philosophy of moral life and the development of wisdom

- Christianity 32 AD – It follows the doctrines of both the Old (the Ten Commandments), and the New Testaments as taught by Jesus and his Disciples

- Islam 570 AD - The philosophy is based on the Quran and the Prophets but mostly on the writings of Muhammad the last Prophet. Depending upon how you conduct your life,

death is either Hell, or an eternally happy after-
life in Heaven

As implied in the above bullets most of the faiths, except
Buddhism, believe that theirs is the only true "Religion"
and people in other religions are all doomed unless they
convert. Many religions overtly try to convert to their
own – the one and only.

Religions of the World

It might be useful to consider how important each of these
religions influence the World and in the United States. This
is not only a function of how they pursue their objectives
but their numbers. The following is their fractional
distribution.

	World	United States
• Christianity -	32%	77%
• Islam - Muhammadism	23%	0.6%
• No Religion -	15%	16%
• Hinduism -	15%	-
• Buddhism -	7%	-
• African Tribes/Other -	6%	3%
• Judaism -	0.2%	1.7%

First on the "No Religion" category, this group can be
divided in three categories. The first, and probably the
largest, are those that haven't thought much about it and
are sufficiently indifferent so that they are not associated
with any of the sub-cults or formal religions. There are the
"Atheists" – "There is no scientific proof of God, but it is
possible". The "Agnostic" has a strong opinion that there

is no God. These non-believers are relatively passive and are not too concerned about other religions if they do not infringe on their personal life.

Most governments of the World have a belief in God which to a greater or lesser extent determines, or at least influences, their laws and policies. In the United States, Courts and many public building are emblazoned with the phrase "In God We Trust" and it is also on all coins and paper money. The President takes the Oath of Office with his hand on the Bible. Clearly, religion has a major affect on the lives of people – sometimes good, other times bad, depending on who is doing the evaluation.

Islam Nations – Muhammadism

The Islam nations of the mid-east are perhaps the most overt in how they pursue Muhammadism, both at home and in foreign countries. Part of the problem is that in the Islam nations there are many sub-cultures, e.g. the ISIS cult, that have their own interpretation of the Qur'an. The concept that death, and the entrance in to "Paradise", is to be desired is imbedded in their philosophy. However, this glorious entrance in to Heaven must be earned, and one of the best ways to earn it is to kill an infidel, the more the better. It is a privilege to be a suicide bomber.

Another characteristic of the Arab nations is that they are both easily offended and if there is a conflict or disagreement the animosity, hatred, and violent reaction goes on between the "warring" parties just about forever. To illustrate this late point, think about Iraq and the Sunni/Shite conflict. Both of these groups believe in Muhammad, but when he died, 632 AD, there was a major disagreement as to who should be his successor and head the religion. The split of the two groups has never been resolved and they still remain enemies.

On the easily offended comment, remember Salman Rushdie. He wrote a novel, "The Satanic Verses", which supposedly mocked the Islamic religion and the government issued an order for his assassination. There were several failed attempts and he fled to the protection of England.

Several cults in the Muslims nations have a strong hatred of other religions, and there for promote violence in most predominately "White" nations including the United States. In addition to the religious view, they blame the United States for much of their internal problems. The Iraq war disrupted the balance of power irritating some groups. The support of the dictator Muammar Caddafi, and any interference in their country, real or imagined, is cause for hatred. On the top of the hatred list is our long support of the Israeli government. Part of this animosity is religion, but also their view of the rest of the World.

Other Religions

Many religions have engaged in violence against the non-believers. Christianity in the Crusades, circa 1200 AD, was not exempt. Most of the uprisings were not World wide but local – sometimes minor between cults but other times more extensive. Buddhism is perhaps one of the only religions that do not actively try to convert others to their own faith.

One of the strange hatreds that exist throughout the World is against the Jewish religion, or is it against the Jewish people. It is strange, because their religion represents only 0.2% of the World's population. This hatred appears to be the result of envy of the large Jewish influence and control of education, business, science, arts, and music. Their leadership in these areas and in others, is way out of proportion to their population percentage. In the elite eastern US universities, Yale/Harvard/Brown, they represent 30% of the faculty. Jews have been awarded 20% of the Nobel Prize Laureates. There are more statistics, but they only reinforce those mentioned. The Jewish population does seem to have greater capability, is it Intelligence or Environment? - this was talked about in the "Education" chapter.

United States

Religion has a major influence in the laws, policies, and activities in most countries, including the United States. I have already mentioned "In God We Trust", but it goes beyond a general philosophy. The stronger advocates of some religions are brainwashed to the point that all individual logic is lost. The "Gospel" is the only and absolute truth – "The World is 6,000 years old"; "I will not take medicine or flue shots for God will protect and look after me": and the list goes on. This kind of thinking may only effect the individual so it is not too important to society, except when it influences laws and education.

Some of these beliefs do infringe on the rights of those who do not have the same view of God and his message, or are nonbelievers. Such issues as the "Right to Life", and influencing the local school board to add "Creationism", a religious philosophy, to the "Science" curriculum in competition with "Darwinism" based on true science.

The "Right to Life" conviction in many States has eliminated programs like "Planned Parenthood" and on many occasions has led to violence. Bombing of the only abortion clinic in the State is an example. Less of an immediate affect, but potentially very important to the future, is the restriction on stem cell research, or even on life saving research on human eggs that are to be discarded.

Anti laws on "Gay Marriage" have been passed, but rulings by the Supreme Court have generally declared them unconstitutional - but keep trying, a new court may change the rule. A strong opinion on these kinds of issues are totally irrational as ether a pro or con position would not make an iota of difference to the way the rest of society would live. Personal rights should trump religion.

Chapter 12

Dysfunctional Governments

Most Nations of the World have "Dysfunctional Governments – only a few would get a "B" or "C" rating.

The consequence of this dysfunction results, or at least contributes, to most of the issues that are discussed in the prior chapters of this book. Some of this dysfunction is not due to the government per se but to the people and their irrational view, or perhaps more kindly, their uneducated judgment on the many issues facing the nation. These are all somewhat damming statements and need a logical defense – read on.

Before we can discuss "Dysfunctional Governments" we need to consider what functions governments should endeavor to develop. This isn't an easy question as it requires not a yes or no answer, but a judgment, an opinion, and judgments vary significantly, depending upon who you ask. There will be clear differences between a Woman/Man, Democrat/Republican, Atheist/Evangelical, Entrepreneur/ Environmentalist, Capitalist/Socialist and the list goes on. With all these internal conflicts it is remarkable that governments function at all.

Philosophically just about everyone agrees that the function of government is to provide the laws, regulations, security, and an environment that provides for a "Good Life" for all of the people, today, tomorrow, and the more distant future for our children and grand-children. The difficult, and nearly impossible, word in this sentence is "All". But there are also difficulties in this simple philosophy – e.g. the balance between today and the future is clearly judgmental and hence open to debate. Not withstanding the "Grayness" in any opinion/choice on the many issues facing the governmental functions, I will comment as to how such functions, or dysfunctions, relate to the ten issues discussed in the prior chapters.

Population

Most governments take a relatively laissez faire approach to population and its "Natural" development – that is the people decide based on a personal view of their future life and that of their children.

This personal view results in wide differences in population growth. In Africa large families are the result of their culture - six to eight or so children, to cope with farming, many early deaths, and support in old age. In the developed countries it is generally about plus or minus two, resulting in small population changes – up or down.

However there have been a number of events that show how government "control" of population becomes dysfunctional. In the 1960s the dictator of Rumania, Nicolae Ceausescu, decided that his country would be stronger if it had a larger population. He banned abortions, the principle method of birth control at that time, and also sex education was stopped. The birth rate doubled and in twenty years the quality of life was drastically down – more poverty, more crime, and the people rebelled. Ceausescu was tried and executed.

Dictatorships are the easiest form of government to control, significantly influence population (e.g. China's one child per family, changed to two) but democracies also have regulations which affect population. In the United States, even after the Roe vs. Wade decision abortion "Regulations" are such that in some States the service is nearly unavailable.

On this issue, the basic question is – "Should the government be involved?" There is not a simple answer, as it depends upon the country and the circumstance.

Consider Africa, we always come back to this troubled region, with its food and water problems, which are greatly exacerbated by one of the highest birth rates in the World. Certainly government promotion of birth control approaches, education, free clinics, pills, would be a step in the right direction, but little of this is happening.

These few paragraphs illustrate a few of the dysfunctions of governments related to population – both action and inaction. However, there does not seem to be much likelihood of any significant change.

Food

There are several areas in the food supply chain that governments are, or should be, involved in:

- A sufficient supply
- Safety and purity
- Is it healthy?

How nations have addressed these, and other related food issues, depends primarily on their industrial development – the countries "Standard of Living". All of the developed nations have done well on safety and are generally wealthy enough to provide for a sufficient supply. As a result of the availability and safety, health is also taken care of, but there is still a question of healthy eating – an individual decision.

Unfortunately, when all types of food are available, people do not always select that which is healthy. United States is a prime example with cheap junk/fast food and 24 ounce sodas – hence one third of the population is overweight, and another one third obese. Both of these conditions lead to national health problems. The Government, mostly States and Cities, have passed a few minor regulations, but should there be more?

In general, the governments of undeveloped counties have done little to encourage or support the supply of sufficient food and this is a major dysfunction of those governments.

Water

The government has two principle functions in the supply of water:

- Deliver clean drinkable water to the home, and in the poorest nations to the neighborhood

- For farming in many regions this may require major infrastructure to get to the crops – dams and aqueducts

To accomplish the first bullet for urban and suburban regions a major source of water is required, a lake or more likely a river and usually at some distance away. A delivery system is required, large tunnels/pipes underground to get to a water treatment plant. There, filtration, chlorination, fluoridation takes place and finally the water is pumped to the distribution grid and the individual dwellings.

All of these steps require a functional government to plan ahead for the future needs and to adequately service the aging infrastructure. In all of the major cities significant potions of the system are over a hundred years old. There are many continuing leaks and more serious failures are common, sometimes disrupting service for a long time.

Dysfunctional governmental action occurs in even the fully industrialized nations. The Flint Michigan story is a case, hopefully not typical, but never the less real. For over two years, 2014 - 2016, after a change in the water supply, it was known that the lead content in the water was dangerously high – many times the government standard. The local administration has dragged it feet and the problem has still not been fully resolved.

In the poorest nations the government may drill a town well, but that is generally their total involvement – no follow up. In the smaller villages there may be a community dug well but certainly no testing to determine whether it is safely drinkable from a toxicity standpoint, or has disease causing bacteria. With no adequate supply or testing, in Africa there are many deaths from contaminated water.

The major water requirements are not for domestic use, or even industrial, but for farming. This water has to come from a local river, a farmer's personal well, or from a more distant source via government aqueducts.

Typically, there is government control, allocation allotments, for the aqueduct water, many times for the river, and rarely for the personal well.

When the farmer's well starts to run dry, the water table level has dropped, the farmer typically drills the well deeper. As regeneration of the aquifer from rain seeping slowly through the ground is less than the water being withdrawn, the level continues to go down. Because these wells are usually very deep, many hundreds of feet, some times thousands, regeneration may take hundreds of years, hence a permanent loss of a natural resource, but profitable for the farmer in the short run.

As these aquifers and rivers are a nation resource it should be the responsibility of a "Functional" government to protect these water asset – and for aquifers only draw out that which rain replaces.

Economics

The difficulty of assessing whether a government is highly functional or dysfunctional as related to economics is the determination of what is a measure of success. Is it gross domestic product per capita, or the rate of growth in the economy, or the standard of living of the people at which level – rich or poor, or is it all of these and more? Overlaying this judgment, what can, should, a government do to develop, or at least influence these many different success criteria and how to chouse between them. Accepting these broad objectives – "What does government do?" and "How do they do it?".

For a good functional government economist nearly all agree that growth, more GNP per capita, is the prime requirement. In their view this growth will trickle down to the population and raise their standard of living.

Even if this "Trickle Down" criteria was absolutely correct which is debatable (e.g. The last 30 years of United States GDP growth) its implementation is subject to many different options which the government controls, or at least influences. These include: Subsidies; Free Trade; Tariffs;

Labor Laws: Income Tax Policy – to name a few of the more important ones. As the pro and con on each of these is debatable there is obviously no right or wrong answer – economics is not a science.

Just to illustrate some of the pros and cons of the options think about the following:

- Free Trade: Pro – It lowers the price of most goods and optimizes World wide manufacturing. Con – In the United States the result has been a major decrease in manufacturing jobs and a huge deficit in the international balance of payment.

- Tariffs: Higher costs of goods and the opposite affect of the above bullet.

- Labor Laws: Pro - Nondiscrimination; Right to Work - but even this has a negative effect as it has drastically lowered union influence, with a result of lower pay; Con – Not raising the minimum wage of $7.25 which is below the poverty level for a full time worker.

- Income Tax: Pro – Lower rates encourage businesses and helping to a degree to keep some manufacturing from going off-shore; Con – The current policy has done nothing to reduce the inequality between the rich and the working poor.

These few example show that it is nearly impossible to decide between "Function" and "Dysfunction" that the government must make on many economic issues

We cannot leave the dysfunctional government with out at least mentioning the last several years of the fiasco in the United States Congress. At the risk of alienating half the readers I can sum it up by a comment about the Republicans – "My way or no way".

Inequality

In nearly all of the countries of the World, and the United States is no exception, there is major inequality between the rich and the poor, even between the rich and the middle class. In addition, racial and religious inequality is also an issue.

Most of the advanced counties have reasonably dealt with the racial and religious inequality, but this issue always needs additional improvement.

However, on economic inequality I believe there is only one word – "Dysfunctional".

Education

The have-not, poor nations, are generally dysfunctional in not providing the facilities, teachers and infrastructure needed. This is primarily due to their poor economy – there is just not enough money to go around.

Another group of nations do not provide a balanced education as they are fully controlled by their religious culture. There is not much hope for a change

Lastly, the fully developed nations all try, but with mixed results. The United States is a prime example, with nearly twice the cost per pupil their average rank, reading/math/science, among the industrialized nations is 20th. This is clearly dysfunctional, but between the educators there are

107

significant differences of opinion as to how to improve education, as very little seems to work.

Health

The industrial nations of the World are doing reasonably well on health issues, except for the United States – at the bottom, twenty-fourth on the list. A major contribution to this poor performance is probably due to the fact that the "Private Health Care" system does not work as well as the Universal Free Health services of all the other nations. The "Private" approach in the United States costs twice as much with poorer results.

The governmental dysfunction in the have not nations is primarily due the poor economic conditions – there is just not enough money. However, it is also debatable whether the current major inequality would be changed, even with a large increase in the nation's gross domestic product.

Global Warming

As developed in the chapter, 97% of the scientists of the World agree that it is real and will result in dire consequences, and this warming is caused by carbon dioxide and methane release to the atmosphere. So the solution is obvious – stop the release.

Obviously stopping releases is not possible as the World could not survive with out the energy for electricity, heating, manufacturing and transportation.

This issue is to how to weigh costs today against the dire consequences, not next year, but a few decades and ultimately the end of the century away. This choice is further exacerbated by the fact that the degree of future problems can not be absolutely determined – How fast and high the oceans will rise? – How the climate change will disrupt farming? – How bad will the future storms and heat waves be?

The "Gray" answer to these and other questions about the future make it difficult to decide how much of today's economy should be directed to the non-polluting energy sources – unfortunately it's a lot of money.

The World is doing something, but is it enough – to be called functional or dysfunctional?

Terrorism

The industrial nations of the World, Europe and the United States are all taking significant actions to prevent, or at least mitigate, the consequences of terrorist acts. Europe has a much more difficult problem because of open borders and high migration, making it easier for terrorists to move around and act. The industrial nations of the World are acting functionally, but I cannot say the same for the mid-east.

In the mid-eastern nations terrorism is imbedded in the culture of hatred and is orders of magnitude more prevalent with often major disastrous results. There is a debate as to whether the many attacks are "Terrorism" or "Civil Strife"- a revolution of sorts. In any case a solution is not likely – "Dysfunctional Government".

Religion

This is a difficult topic to assess functionality to. By definition religions are a personal issue and if they follow their own charter, the Bible, the Koran, the Old Testament, they are not dysfunctional. That is not to say that there are not differences of interpretation of the charter, but this is within that religion's members and should be internally resolved.

The outside World, not of that religion, may have strong feelings about the rationality or practices of some religious groups, but this an external view. The quarrel, if there is one, is with the "normal" functions of that religion if it infringes on the rights of others.

Chapter 13

Conclusions

If you have arrived at this point in the book you are probably frustrated, mad, worrying, or all of these. The World, and the nations of the World, have many serious problems, issues, that action should be initiated to modify, improve, or eliminate the issue. How much can, or will be done is a serious question. I certainly do not have an answer but the following are my thought on the eleven issues discussed in the preceding chapters.

Population

The World population is probably the most critical issue that the World faces. Population drives everything that is needed for life – food, land, housing, energy, and all of the other things current populations demand.

The population in 2100 cannot be known, but he United Nation nominal estimate is 11 billion. However, the possible range is unbelievable – a negligible decrease from the current 7.3 billion to a top at 17 billion. If we ever came close to this highest level of population I fear that the resources of the earth would be tapped beyond what is possible. Food, energy, water, land would be in such short supply that both civil and national wars could easily develop. That will certainly bring the population down. Malthusian philosophy may still be alive.

Even at the current population level we are depleting many resources - water, arable farm land, and the forests of the World. Some "Experts" believe that the earth can permanently and reasonably support only about 5 billion people. It is not going to happen, so let us hope they are wrong.

Food

There is already a shortage, to the point of malnutrition and even starvation, in the undeveloped nations, and to a lesser extent in the developing, nations of the World.

The technology of modern farming and food distribution could be brought to the developing nations to improve their food availability. The issue is whether it can be possible. Implementation of current farming technology requires a lot of capital – the machines, irrigation, fertilizer, and the infrastructure. The poor nations just do not have it unless they are able to boost their economy to a higher level. Most of the economic development in, Africa, Southeast Asia, follows the usual corporate view of early profits – not a plan for the future. World organizations, like the United Nations, think about these issues but generally do not have the resources to implement significant actions. Let us hope that there will be some improvements or there will be more food shortages with dire consequences.

Water

In the rivers and lakes of the World there is enough water to meet our needs, but it may not be conveniently located so it takes capital to develop a delivery system. This will certainly be a problem for Africa where even a minimal supply is not available in many regions. As the population increases there will be more farming with a demand for irrigation that will exacerbate the shortage.

There will certainly be conflicts on water rights of rivers and this could be both within a nation, States rights in the United States, and between nations as many rivers are international. As nations strive for upward mobility there will be an increase in water use.

Land represents a more complicated issue again significantly related to food and the changing diets – fewer grains and more meats. As has been shown in America, high meat consumption greatly increases the need for more farm land as well as water, and in many countries adequate arable farm land is in short supply.

Economics

The key issue here is whether the philosophy of most economists that there must be greater growth in the economy, both World-wide and in the United States, is either valid or possible in the 21st century.

In the World, growth is desirable and certainly possible, as the developing nations increase their Gross Domestic Product and improve their standard of living. In the latter half of the 20th century the growth in the World averaged about 4 to 5% - quite high by historical standards. It has dropped in the 21st century to around 2%.

Like the World, the United States had an amazing growth of GDP in the 20th century, a result of the most inventive century in history, and that would be impossible to duplicate. The current rate is on the order of 2% per year. Even this rate may not be sustainable for at our current 300 **Q** per billion people how much more can the nation consume.

A discouraging component of the US economy that is not in good shape is manufacturing. The lion's share of our growth in the last 30 years has been in the service industry while manufacturing has dropped dramatically. The Trade Balance deficit in manufactured goods rose from a nominal $30 billion per year to $500 billion in this same time frame, and it seems to be locked in. This level of trade deficit can not be sustained in to the future.

Inequality

Inequality is a result of several differing forces. The force most considered is economic inequality – the difference in income between the rich and the poor, and this inequality drives others. If you are poor your standard of living is marginal – inadequate food, less or minimal education, less chance for upward mobility, and certainly none of the "luxuries" of current living.

Much of these inequalities could be improved by a nation's increase in gross domestic product, but this increase must be distributed in some reasonable degree between the poor/ destitute and the rich. In the richest nation, the United States, essentially all of the large growth in the GDP of the last 30 years went to the rich and supper rich – the middle class stayed about even and the poor became poorer.

Strangely, baste on past histories inequality does not generally bring about major riots or civil wars. Uprisings are generally originated in a smaller cohesive groups that do not go very far – e.g. "Occupy Wall Street".

There will always be inequality resulting from a spectrum of jobs – a trash collector, a truck driver, a teacher will all have different income levels. This difference in income automatically results in inequality of living. However, the differences must have some rationale and the lower paying jobs must provide for an acceptable life. The incredible differences in both income and wealth between the poor, or even the middle class, and the supper rich, is not acceptable.

Education

The fundamental purpose of education is to prepare a person for a better, happier, and more useful life. Training/education to prepare a person for a better job is clearly an objective to sought, and this also leads to a more useful life. To think logically should also be an objective, but in many cases this falls by the wayside, replaced by education by "Rote".

The ability to read well can be a major step toward a happier life. Books are informative, relaxing, funny, moving, and in some cases challenging. Reading is a great was to spend any spare time you might have.

Unfortunately, many nations do not do well in education, some because of financial reasons, but many others because we just do not know how to teach well. Among the industrial nations and developing industrial nations of the World United States ranks poorly – 15th in reading, 26th in math, and 18th in science. This is in spite of having one of the highest cost per pupil in the World. There are studies from here to there with wide differences of opinion but with no good results to date.

In many nations of the World, religion dictates what is taught, and this is generally counter to a broader and more useful education. Even in the United States, a number of States driven by religion restrict the teaching of science because that course would include a study of Darwinian Theory.

Health

The industrial nations with universal health care are doing reasonably well. There is always room for improvement.

The United States, on the other hand, clearly needs to identify why health care costs twice as much, and with poorer results. Free universal health care would be great and probably reduce costs and improve the health of the nation. The likelihood of this happening is just about zero.

Global Warming

This is an issue that is both real and the consequences will affect all nations of the World. Climate change will be World wide with warmer weather moving north, more rain in some regions, drought in others, which will cause crops to be changed and farmers to move. These changes will be extremely rapid compared to pre-historic changes, but will probably be slow enough to be manageable but upsetting.

The other change, already measurable, is the rising level of the sea - now only a few inches, but estimated to be several feet by the end of the century. This will seriously cause many sea shore areas around the World to be evacuated, and a few nations, e.g. Bangladesh, will be destroyed. The economic impact will be huge.

How bad will this climate change be and the sea level rise is yet to be determined as these changes are a function of how well the nations of the earth can reduce the release of green-house gasses. Even if these releases were instantly reduced to zero, much damage has already been done and the temperatures of the World would still continue to rise for some period of time with its associate problems.

The World nations have finally gotten the message but how effective their actions will be in the next few decades is yet to be determined. To be even partially successful all coal fueled electric generating station would have to be shut down and replaced with wind, solar and with a major contribution of new nuclear power stations. This is in addition to reducing all of the other releases – primarily transportation. The others, industrial, residential, and farming are much more difficult to deal with, particularly as the World gross domestic product inevitably continues upward. Good luck!

Terrorism

Terrorism is a major threat in many area of the World, primarily in the mid-east, but not in the United States. The public and the media have a different view, but this is not supported by the evidence. The facts are that since 9/11, terrorist deaths in America have averaged only 34 per year, a number that would never be noticed if it wasn't high lighted with blazing headlines and continuous TV coverage. Other daily risks, automobile deaths at 34,000 per year, gun at 31,000, accidental at 130,000 are accepted without a murmur.

Our government security system has been very good and hopefully it will continue with its excellent record. It does have a problem identifying an individual, or a few person group, as there are potentially thousands of individuals that are in this category. Hopefully, the consequences of their actions will continue to be relatively small.

There is one potential future disaster which would move 9/11 into insignificance, and that is a nuclear bomb attack. It is conceivable that a mid-east terrorist, a group like ISIS, could steal, or otherwise acquire, a nuclear weapon. Let us hope for the best.

Religion

Religion is a significant influence on the laws, customs, and actions of most nations of the World. Many of religious beliefs are useful and desirable – "Love thy Neighbor" - "Peace". However, many religions tend to be self important to the point of violence - if you are not one of us. Other religious views, more mildly tend to influence, sometimes demand, that other persons not or their faith conform to their view of life. This "My View", drives laws and education, to the exclusion of the rights and views of others. Even in liberal United States, in many States religion has influenced public education and nearly forbids personal choice in such issues as "Right to Life" – even if it is my own.

With the views and philosophy of most religions in place for hundreds to even thousands of years, I do not see much a change in the future. There may be a modest shift to a more liberal view in the western countries, but certainly not in the mid-east.

Epilogue

I am sure you do not agree with many of my thoughts as developed in this book but I hope that it has at least stimulated your thinking about these eleven "ISSUES". It may even have changed some of your views.

Most of these issues are continuously evolving so that the ultimate consequences are yet to be determined. Population, particularly in Africa, along with food is a major issue for the rest of this century. Global warming is here and will get worse, as I do not foresee sufficient success in the difficult task of reducing the release of green-house gasses.

Finally, on economics, the United States must learn to live with a very modest increase in the gross domestic product, and develop a solution to a further loss of jobs as automation and robotics become more prevalent. Ultimately there must be a leveling of the major inequality of income and wealth between the lower half of the population and the supper rich.

Let us hope for the World there is progress toward a reasonable, rational solution to all of these, and other issues.

About the Author

Robert William Kupp is a graduate Chemical Engineer who became a Nuclear Engineer after his work on the Manhattan Atom Bomb project during World War II in Oak Ridge, Tennessee. From that nuclear beginning, Mr. Kupp's full time career was in the development of civilian nuclear power, its economics, its fuel, and safety. He was also an Adjunct Professor in Nuclear Engineering at New York Polytechnic University.

After his retirement, in addition to more reading, music, oil painting, and some traveling he wrote two books. The first, an autobiography, "A Nuclear Engineer in the Twentieth Century" which discussed not only his working career, but his youth, home life, the island of Nantucket and sailing. His second book, "ENERGY – A Solution", is a laissez faire approach to energy's future – with a combination of conservation, wind, solar and nuclear.

This book includes some of his energy thoughts in the Chapter on "Global Warming" an issue that will affect every nation in the World

Printed in the United States
By Bookmasters